Encountering God

ENCOUNTERING GOD

Christian Faith in Turbulent Times

Andrew Purves
Charles Partee

Westminster John Knox Press
Louisville, Kentucky

Scripture quotations from the New Revised Standard Version
of the Bible are copyright © 1989
by the Division of Christian Education of the National Council
of the Churches of Christ in the U.S.A.
and are used by permission.

Scripture quotations from the Revised Standard Version
of the Bible are copyright © 1946, 1952, 1971
by the Division of Christian Education of the National Council
of the Churches of Christ in the U.S.A.
and are used by permission.

Book design by Sharon Adams
Cover design by Pamela Poll Graphic Design

First edition

Published by Westminster John Knox Press
Louisville, Kentucky

This book is printed on acid-free paper that meets the
American National Standards Institute Z39.48 standard. ∞

PRINTED IN THE UNITED STATES OF AMERICA
00 01 02 03 04 05 06 07 08 09 — 10 9 8 7 6 5 4 3 2 1

Library of Congress Cataloging-in-Publication
Data is on file at the Library of Congress,
Washington, D.C.

ISBN 0-664-22242-0

This book is dedicated to
Catherine Johanna Purves
and
Margaret McClure Partee,
with our love and gratitude.

Contents

Foreword

This book began at the dinner table late in the evening after other guests had gone home. The conversation turned to one of our favorite subjects, the loss of doctrinal clarity in the contemporary church. Perhaps a trifle exasperated with the predictability of the topic, both our wives lovingly but firmly suggested that our time and energy might be better employed in addressing the problem rather than fussing about it. "Why," they said, "don't you write a book together?" A book, jointly written, sounded like a good idea. We would like to thank Margaret and Cathy for their good idea, assuming they had little notion how much work the project would involve!

A theological friendship takes a long time to build. Such a relationship involves a generally shared perspective on matters of Christian faith, and also includes trust and affection that develop substantially over time. We met twenty years ago when asked to serve together on a committee dealing with church issues that focused on the doctrine of Jesus Christ. Seventeen years ago we became, and remain, colleagues on the faculty of Pittsburgh Theological Seminary. In addition to many dinner conversations, we have learned to compete and cooperate on the tennis court in weekly doubles matches for nearly two decades. Some time back we began to pass drafts of writing-in-progress to one another for editorial counsel. These suggestions were sometimes longer than the original essay! Sharing the work of author and editor seemed natural. Since then we have often written and spoken as a team.

Writing a book together we discovered is not a fifty-fifty proposition, but more like each writing 75 percent. Coauthoring is also an exercise in humility. Each of us accepted the assignment to begin the draft of various chapters, but the other was expected to do vigorous editing. Some of these chapters were rewritten so many times we can no longer identify individual authorship. Often one of us would say, "Here it is as far as I could go. You finish it." The "you finish it" became a kind of recurring refrain over the final few months of our writing. Although some pieces are readily identifiable "Partee stories" and "Purves stories," every chapter has been jointly written.

The unifying theme of this book is the single, saving Lordship of Jesus Christ. Although only one chapter bears that title, the Lordship of Christ and our union with him are essential to every basic doctrine in Christian faith. In fact, this relationship defines what makes a doctrine a Christian doctrine. We have selected matters for discussion that are central for Christian faith. In some cases there is controversy in which we have interest. Other doctrines could be included no doubt; the doctrines presented here could not be omitted. Under the conviction of faith, we present basic beliefs for these turbulent times.

The two of us have been teaching theology for nearly half a century, but we remain pastors at heart. This book is written for the church with a pastoral rather than academic purpose. We intend a pastoral emphasis, both in the subjects selected and the manner of the treatment. Autobiographical and pastoral stories not only illustrate the discussion, but in most cases they inform the doctrinal discussion that follows. We have written from our hearts and heads to the hearts and heads of the people of God, trying to be both faithful and reasonable. As far as two theologians could manage, the book is free from technical terms and theological jargon. We offer it with the prayer that God will use these basic beliefs for the growth and enrichment of the people of God.

Writing a book is strange, hard, often stimulating, and always adventurous work. Writing a book together is an especially companionable experience. For us the chief joy, however, has been the affirmation of faith in our Lord Jesus Christ in the fellowship of the shared ministry that produced this volume.

1

Encountering God

The Prophet Isaiah

"In the year that King Uzziah died I saw the Lord sitting upon a throne, high and lifted up, and his train filled the temple" (6:1). The content of this experience included God's holiness and glory, and Isaiah's own sinfulness. However, notice that Isaiah did not claim to see a vision. He claimed to see the Lord!

The Apostle Paul

As Saul of Tarsus approached the city of Damascus, "suddenly a light from heaven flashed around him. He fell to the ground and heard a voice saying to him, 'Saul, Saul, why do you persecute me?' He asked, 'Who are you, Lord?' The reply came, 'I am Jesus.'" (Acts 9:3–5) The Apostle Paul did not merely claim to hear a voice. He claimed to hear the voice of Jesus, risen from the dead.

As ministers of the Word and sacraments, we begin our book with two famous biblical narratives of people encountering God. These accounts could be multiplied many times by other stories of lives disordered or reordered after encounters with God. Augustine, the North African Latin Father, in the garden heard a child's voice, "Take and read." The history of the West changed forever in that single event of Augustine's conversion when he picked up the Bible and read

1

from Romans 13:13–14.[1] Blaise Pascal, the seventeenth-century French mathematician and philosopher, encountered God in a fiery experience while reading the seventeenth chapter of John's Gospel, and wrote in his famous *Memorial* the words "God of Abraham, God of Isaac, God of Jacob, not of the philosophers and *savants.*" A century later, John Wesley had his heart strangely warmed listening to a reading from Martin Luther. This event led to the birth of Methodism. In modern times, Thomas Merton encountered God in a hotel room in Rome and later in a Cuban chapel. This erratic young man became in time a Trappist monk and a great spiritual teacher. Mother Teresa encountered God among the poor in Calcutta, leading to a life of ministry to the least of them as she saw the faces of Christ in the face of the poor. With one voice the Bible and Christian tradition affirm that God encounters us.

Of course, ordinary Christians know they live in God's presence, but sometimes and on special occasions they, too, encounter God. Since the discussion of basic beliefs is a confessional activity, we thought setting aside academic impartiality and including our own witness to encounter with God would be not only honest but helpful.

Andrew Purves

My encounter with God is a story of the extraordinary amid the ordinary. I had left school at age sixteen with a sense of lassitude toward formal education. Although I had forsaken a conventional educational route, I was working in an accountant's office and successfully pursuing studies by correspondence. Along with the usual pastimes of a youngster of my age, I was also keenly interested in philosophical, moral, and political issues. I even held office in a political party. My family life was secure, I had a wonderful company of friends, and I had a deep sense of my roots and good hopes for my future. For me these were exciting times to be idealistic and young in Britain, with the hope of a new Labor government later in 1964 and the sense of expectation in the air. On the surface, my life was full of challenge, and I eagerly awaited my future.

I had not grown up in the church, and Christian faith and the Church of Scotland were very far from my thinking and practice. Yet on a Sunday evening in March 1964, in my parents' living room, God intervened in a totally unexpected and extraordinary way. The picture is still vivid in my memory. I rose to leave the room and stopped suddenly by my mother's chair. There was no crisis in my life at the time, but one was about to happen. Rather strangely, I said to my mother, "I'm bored with my life." Looking back, I am not sure why I said that or even that it was true. My mother had not attended church much at all since she was a Roman Catholic schoolgirl in Presbyterian Edinburgh. I had seen her in worship only at weddings and funerals, yet altogether surprisingly she replied, "Why don't you go to church next Sunday?" To this day I have wondered where on earth (or heaven?) these words came from. One can only wonder at the mystery of God's grace that works its redeeming purpose in the deep wisdom of a mother's love for her child.

My mother's words created an odd and frankly disturbing resonance during the ensuing week. Somewhat nervously I attended church the following Sunday. I sat on a back pew (of course!) amid the scattering of people mostly older than I, anticipating boredom, yet with a hint of anxiety, and hoping nobody would notice me. The second act of a mischief-making God was about to change my life forever. The minister (wearing traditional Scottish Protestant clergy vestments) ascended into the pulpit. He gripped the edge of the pulpit and in a firm voice said: "Let us worship God."

Those words came cannonading over the end of the pulpit and tore into my teenage head with a mighty roar. I cannot say that I heard the voice of God as an aural noise. I can say that I heard the voice of God in an interior way, invading my life, demanding my attention in a manner I could not avoid, turning my ordered life upside down. I knew immediately with utter conviction and clarity that God had called me to be a minister. I was called to preach the gospel before I was even a Christian. This encounter with God is the initiating and defining moment that has given shape, direction, and meaning to my life. In the encounter with God, God disordered my life.

Charles Partee

According to our family memory, all our ancestors, as far back as we knew, were Christian people. Certainly my father and mother and their parents established Christian homes without considering the possibility of other options. Therefore, being surrounded by Christian nurture (including prayer, scripture, and worship), I neither expected nor required anything else for my pilgrimage.

Every summer brought revivals to some of the other local churches in my little town. The sermons were usually passionate and the emotions seldom restrained. I often attended but was too inhibited to participate. Nevertheless, in my early teens, I was not surprised to discover the clear conviction that I should be a minister. I was too humble to think this was my decision. I rather figured that God, respecting my quiet ways, had called me by stripping away all the attractions of any other possible life's work. I did not expect to be very good at ministry, but I knew I would be happy engaged in it. Thus, I began with deep joy to prepare.

During the hours and years of preparation, a day arrived when I was to appear for "coming under the care of the presbytery." Dignified elders and ministers assembled to conduct the business of the kingdom of God, of which one small agenda item was me. Summoned to the front of the sanctuary I was seated on the first bench to the left of the moderator, feeling considerable stress, lack of sleep, and the need for a quiet cup of coffee in a corner somewhere else.

As the solemn words of the liturgy began to roll over me, I started to sob uncontrollably. I was only a little embarrassed because, while nothing like this had ever happened to me before, there was nothing I could do about it. The moderator interrupted the service to say to the congregation, "This man has received a call to ministry." I only just stopped myself from responding out loud, "You're damned right he has!" I was amazed at the emphatic nature of that unuttered sentence because (at the time) the word *damn* was entirely restricted to my reading and hearing vocabulary.

To this point I thought I understood what was going on with me. However, and to my most intense surprise, as the service resumed and I began to come back under normal control, I looked up to my right into the ceiling vault of the church. I saw there a smiling face (in color) that I immediately identified as my Lord, Jesus Christ. The message that burst with absolute certainty into my mind's ear was, "I am pleased, and I will be with you always."

Until now I have never told this story since I do not know exactly what to make of it. Actually, I have never tried to make anything of it. And, frankly, I do not want to make anything of it now. I just report the event because I was there and it happened to me. I have always remembered this experience as the moment my life was reordered.

Avoiding Misunderstanding

This book does not analyze encounters with God. Our subject is not ourselves, nor anybody else for that matter. Our discipline is not the psychology of religious experience. Rather, our discipline is theology, and our subject is God. We want to call attention, therefore, to the fact that *the discussion of Christian faith ultimately depends on the reality of the subject to which they refer.* At some level a blind person may be able to discuss the color "red." An unmarried person perhaps can discuss wedded love. Perhaps military science could be taught in a classroom from books a teacher had read, but more likely "A fellow . . . / That never set a squadron in the field, / Nor the division of a battle knows [will demonstrate] mere prattle, without practice, / Is all his soldiership" (Othello, I, 1.21–23, 26–27).

Certainly atheists and agnostics use the word "God," but for them it is a general noun. For Christians, however, "God" is a personal name. In fact, God is the one who encounters us and makes us believers. As believers we speak of the One whom we have met, whom we know, and whom we love, worship, and serve. This chapter suggests that encounter with God leads to adoration of God, which in turn leads to reflection on faith in God.

In the wonder of God's providence, God does not deal with everyone in the same way. Curiously for some people the order is reversed: they first become believers and then God encounters them in a special way. Moreover, for some people the presence of God in their lives is so steady and gentle that the language of encounter may seem inappropriate to their experience. Those who grow up in the faith, "children of the covenant," may never know a time when they were not confident of God's presence. Certainly confirmations from and encounters with God can be quietly woven into the tapestry of faithful lives. Thus "presence" may be an alternative term to "encounter." In any case, to suppose that God is not free to deal with us in a variety of ways would be a serious mistake. Nevertheless, the subject of theology is not our experience of our treatment by God. The real subject is God who deals with each of us singly and as a community. The proper focus is God, not us. However conceived and articulated, all Christians know that God deals with them.

God's initial and personal relation to each of us and our relation to God in response are immensely complicated topics.[2] Christians believe that God as creator relates to all peoples (Rom. 1:18–23). However, without trying to analyze in detail the knowledge of God our creator and redeemer, God clearly does not relate to everyone in the same way. God meets us as we need to be met. God respects our categories, the frames of meaning that we use to make sense of the world. God acts within our personal histories in ways that do not violate us and that affirm each person's individuality. However, while God may start there, God does not leave us there. Some people need to be dramatically awakened out of their pagan sleep. Others just need to be nudged along with a gentle encouragement. Each encounter with God is unique, and each encounter with God is both disordering and reordering because it is the same God who acts and to the same end—our salvation and lives that are to become holy through faithfulness. For this reason we cannot make our own experience of God prescriptive for others. Neither dare we try to fit the understanding of God into the description of our own encounter with God. Because of the individualness with which each of us encounters God, we must not confuse our experience of God with the God we experience. God is greater than all our personal stories put together.

Our present point is that while Christian faith arises in the minds and hearts of faithful persons and the faithful community, faith does not originate there. To think that Christian faith is ultimately about how faithful Christians are to Christ rather than how faithful Christ is to Christians is a serious misunderstanding. Because God is faithful, God encounters us and is involved in disordering and reordering our lives. Thus, as Francis Thompson put it, God, like the hound of heaven, chases us down the labyrinthine ways of our lives. Encountering God changes us by disordering and reordering our lives according to God's purpose. The subject of faith is not our individual experience but God.

Seeking Assurance

In this skeptical age the conviction of God's presence in our lives raises two immediate problems that might be called the "How" question and the "Who" question. First, we ask how do we know we encounter the living God? Sigmund Freud, for example, tells us there is no God to encounter. For that reason Freud insists humans project their fears on the universe and create the God they need. Second, we ask who is the God who encounters us? That is, what moves our experience beyond the generically divine to the specifically Christian knowledge of God? To these profound questions we can offer only brief answers.

First, every personal assertion is privileged in the sense that I alone can know if I am too hot or too cold. At the same time these claims can be variously explained. For example, illness or refusal to wear a coat on a cold morning could account for a chill. The presentation of supporting evidence differs depending on the claims made. Thus, an assertion that a chair is in the room has a simple demonstration. On the other hand, the affirmation that "I am in love" is more difficult to prove to a skeptic's satisfaction. The claim to encounter God is impossible to prove. That we are deceived and what seemed to be God was a psychological effect of our needs or even the biological effect of our diet is always possible. We must recognize that on occasion human beings force events into preexisting categories of their minds. Of course, our interpretation of an experience as an encounter with God might then be quite in error, but then so could my conviction that I am in love, and so on.

In this connection, it is important to note that some persons who call themselves "theologians" actually believe that the term "God" refers only to a special way of understanding the human situation. In the modern period, the philosopher Immanuel Kant sought to defend Christianity by basing its claims not on God, but upon ethics.[3] In response, Friedrich Schleiermacher offered a psychological defense of Christianity based upon the "feeling of absolute dependence." In each case the intent was to refer correctly to a divine being, but the result was a focus on human being. According to Kant two things filled him with awe: the starry heavens above and the moral law within. We certainly affirm the natural and moral order, but we deny that God is restricted to either. Theology confesses the sovereign freedom of God. Otherwise theology becomes only a way of speaking about ourselves and our world. If encountering God is a special kind of self-encounter, then theology is really anthropology without remainder.

In opposition to this basic trend in liberal theology we appeal to the central message of the New Testament and the broad stream of Christian tradition: encountering God reveals a reality other than ourselves who meets us, and who through the encounter disorders and reorders our lives. Further, we profess that we can know this Other who interferes in our lives, not merely as a grand idea, but in a personal way as Lord. No more ultimate basis exists for ratifying the reality of the encounter with God than the encounter itself. This fact will keep theologians humble because they obviously do not control their subject. They can only testify to the God who converts the mind (Rom. 12:2) and calls all Christians to lives of faithful service. In this way, the shape of Christian life gives some public evidence for one's understanding and commitment to God. Even so, because encounters with God are individual and nonrepeatable in nature, they may be reported but not demonstrated. They remain personal, private, and real.

Second, the identity of God likewise admits no simple, formulaic answer. In fact, whether speaking of our knowledge of nature, of ourselves, and especially of God, the precise relation between fact and interpretation, or between experience and interpretation, is notoriously difficult to unravel. Christians believe that the true God is revealed to Israel and is incarnate in Jesus Christ. Generally—but not always—interpretation accompanies event. Sometimes, however, especially in missionary contexts, an encounter occurs that is only later understood. Nevertheless, whatever the case, Christian faith teaches that the encounter with God is an encounter with Jesus Christ because God is revealed in and through Jesus Christ. The Word of God became flesh and dwelt among us, full of grace and truth (John 1:14). The Christian encounter with God requires the confession that "Jesus Christ is Lord" (Phil. 2:11).

In whatever way God deals with us, the fact is that God deals with us. God moves into our lives one way or another and changes who we would otherwise be. This encounter with God is not a neutral experience but instead is an experience that ruffles, disturbs, and disquiets us, or just quietly changes our lives. The point is that encountering

God changes us. And however it comes, this encounter provokes—indeed demands—a response. Thus, the encounter with God and the response to God belong together. Individuals, and sometimes even groups (e.g. , at Pentecost in Acts 2), report encounters with God, but no one can offer an adequate definition of them. They are convictional and nonnegotiable. Nevertheless, we can observe that encountering God produces two results. The first result is worship and the second is the renewal of thinking. Encounter with God leads to adoration, which leads to reflection.

An early teacher in the church, Evagrius Ponticus, once said that "a theologian is one whose prayer is true." Worship of God and knowledge of God belong together in response to the God who disorders and then reorders our lives. Worship comes first because everything else flows from our adoration of the God who encounters us in Jesus Christ our Lord. As faith seeks understanding so does adoration require our reflection on and living of the amended and obedient life.

The Renewal of Worship

Encountering God requires that all of life will henceforth be lived to the praise and glory of God. According to the Westminster Shorter Catechism (answer one), "Man's chief end is to glorify God." Thus Christian faith and life gives first place to the glory of God. Before we "can enjoy Him forever," we must "glorify God." The glory of God protects our understanding of God and our living the Christian life by keeping God in God's place and us in ours. The first act of faith, then, is worship by which we give God the glory.

The point is, if the glory of God is not our immediate focus and concern, something else is, and therein lies the problem with so much modern Protestantism. The "something else" positioned in the center is ourselves. We may trace this development back to René Descartes, the seventeenth-century French philosopher, whose famous statement "I think, therefore I am" made the self-reflective thinking mind the center of all knowledge. By the use of this philosophical method, the modern world is the self-centered world. But people instructed by scripture know that the problem goes back much farther, to the Garden of Eden. The first couple, Adam and Eve, in committing the first sin felt the consequence of putting their own wills above the will of

God. For then their eyes were opened, and they both knew they were naked. Instead of peace and community with God, they instead knew fear and shame before God. (Gen. 3:7–10) Putting second things first always leads to disaster. Placing ourselves rather than the glory of God at the center of life led and leads to the great human predicament, namely, fear and shame rather than joy and peace through communion with God. Misplacing God and putting ourselves in God's place is certainly one way to understand the nature of sin. Worship is the great act of reorientation by which we ensure that God is in God's place. Adoration is the proper response to God's glory.

Recognizing that our words and actions are responsive, not determinative, means that worship of God is not primarily about us and our experiences of the holy. Worship is about the praise of God in all things. Because God has encountered us in his glory, we are disordered and reordered, driven from our adoration of ourselves—which is sin—to praise of God. The primary subject and object of worship is God and God's glory. Worship is not about our spiritual aspirations nor our religious feelings. However many useful pages may issue from academic reflection, the Christian faith finds its power not in the private context of a scholar's book room, but in the public worship of the encountering God.

The question, "What worship does God require of us?" takes us to the heart of the doctrine of God, thereby exposing our extraordinary confusion. To worship God rightly we are forced to ask: Who is God? The answer is not found by attending to what humans like to do, but by attending to what is worthy of and appropriate for offering to Almighty God insofar as God has given us the means through Word and sacraments. At least in Reformed theology, worship cannot be defined pragmatically as meeting spiritual and emotional needs in order to achieve success in the ecclesiastical marketplace. Pious worship is worship that is theologically faithful to the God of glory.

Whether we are conservative or modernist in our worship tastes, whether we prefer older or newer liturgies or some blend of the two, the primary question is: Does this worship seek to honor the glory of God? Or, to put it another way: In worship, are we attempting to please God or attempting to please ourselves? All of us need to engage in critical, repentant reflection here, because what has always been done may just be old sins validated by time. At the same time, new ways may just be new sins that appeal to modern sensibilities.

In the midst of the pain and confusion over worship that is found everywhere across the church, clearly worship must declare God's glory (Ps. 96:3). Anything else is an abomination. Entering the third Christian millennium, and in the context of serious discussions over unity and diversity, obedience to God requires many things of the modern church. But whatever our diversities may be, our unity consists in the recognition of the divine glory before which all God's people fall to their knees, confessing "the only wise God be glory for evermore through Jesus Christ! Amen." (Rom. 16:27)

The Renewal of Thinking

Worshiping God also requires using the mind to guide the service of our lives in faithfulness to the mission of the gospel. Although we can never fully succeed, we must still try to understand and serve the God who chooses to encounter us and to receive our adoration. Obviously our concern is with understanding and serving God, not with understanding and serving ourselves. It may be that understanding can seek faith, but the usual pattern is that existing faith seeks possible understanding. That is, we seek knowledge of the God in whom we have faith that we may serve God faithfully with our lives. The reality of God always precedes faith, and faith normally precedes the task of understanding. (See John 6.69: "We have come to believe and know.") In its most basic sense the fact of faith is nonnegotiable because no reference exists to which we can appeal to validate faith, except God, who being steadily or suddenly encountered, or both, produces it. The process of understanding for the life of service, on the other hand, is continually developing in a variety of ways. This book intends to advance the process of faithful reflection.

Encountering God means that God commands our attention—in one way or another. But we have insisted as strongly as we can that our growth in knowledge of God is not by way of us thinking about ourselves. We grow in knowledge of God by learning about God, because God has given us the Word of God, first in God's covenantal history with Israel and second in the incarnation of the Word in Jesus Christ. To these, respectively, the Old and New Testaments give unique and authoritative witness. Theology as the discipline of reflecting upon God is always in some basic way biblical theology. At every turn the Bible guides our thoughts and reflections as we seek to understand ever more deeply the Lord to whom the scriptures bear witness.

Further, we are not the first students who seek knowledge of God. For two thousand years men and women have reflected upon the Word of God, and the church has periodically affirmed certain insights into and formulations of faith as having special authority. We read and study the scriptures and do our theology in the company of a great cloud of witnesses who have taught faithfully the meaning of the scriptures and a truthful knowledge of God. While we seek knowledge of God for today, we turn humbly also to learn from past teachers. To that end, we stand within the family of Reformed Christians for whom the Geneva churchman John Calvin holds a special place of honor as a faithful interpreter of the Word of God.

The Christian beliefs that are the subject of this book receive their importance as they foster correct understanding of the God to whom they are offered as a witness. In other words, doctrinal reflection on Christian faith and life is a deeply humble testimony to the Holy God because the word "God" is not an abstract noun but the personal name of the One who encounters us, enters into relationship with us, and calls us in all things to live to His glory. The reality of God is the final problem for philosophy but the first certainty for theology. The twentieth-century philosopher Karl Jaspers affirms this point when he writes, "No philosophy can comprehend religion either as a historic phenomena or as a living faith. Philosophical thinking confronts religion as an ever-perplexing attitude, a weight it cannot lift or a resistance it cannot surmount."[4] Shakespeare's Hamlet said the same thing in fewer words,

> There are more things in Heaven and earth, Horatio,
> Than are dreamt of in your philosophy
>
> (I.v. 166–67).

2

The Mystery of Faith

No one who grows up in America can escape all contact with revivals. Revivals had a powerful impact on the American frontier, and they continue in another form on television today. In my early teens, before I could drive a car, I was taken on a hot summer day to a Billy Graham evangelistic crusade at a football stadium in Memphis, Tennessee. A platform was set up in the middle of the field and one side of the stadium was packed. After some music to warm us up, the preaching began. Billy Graham did not say anything I had not already heard in my teenage life, but I had never been in a worship service with so many people. I was both impressed by the group emotion and resistant to it. The central message, as I understood it, was "Have faith in God." What bothered me, even as a kid, about Billy Graham's message and others like it was that he seemed to me to overemphasize human choice and underemphasize divine grace. God's grace appeared to be a prize held out for one to grab rather than a gift lovingly and directly bestowed. Certainly Christians want to affirm human freedom and responsibility, but as Reformed Christians we also want to affirm divine love and sovereignty.

Faith is a central fact of the Christian life. According to Mark, Jesus' very first words asserted the requirement of faith: "The time is fulfilled, and the kingdom of God is at hand; repent, and believe in the gospel." (1:15) Christians can never have too much faith in God, but many of us believe that our desire for faith comes within the context of God's prior and abiding love for us. That is, our decision for God

13

is motivated by God's decision for us. We cannot contemplate a time when we stood outside God's grace and indeed God's special grace for each one of us.

Here's the tension: Having faith is so central to our Christian life that we must think carefully about it, but faith is so complicated that it will always remain a mystery. Of some eighty chapters in John Calvin's *Institutes of the Christian Religion* the longest is devoted to explaining faith, thus indicating the importance and complexity of this subject. Calvin locates his discussion of faith about halfway through the *Institutes*, though we raise the topic in chapter 2 because we believe faith is more misunderstood in our time than in Calvin's.

We understand faith to be a gift of God and not simply a human work. Many of us misunderstand the faith issue today because modern people have a serious "I" problem. We tend to accept our own reality more readily and easily than we do the reality of God. Thus our thinking begins with ourselves, not God. The question, "Does God exist?" appears to modern people a legitimate subject of inquiry, but the question, "Do I exist?" seems ridiculous because the answer is so obvious. The declaration "Glory to God in the highest" has in some minds been replaced by "Glory to Humankind in the Highest."

It might help to include a philosophical and historical reference point here. The shift from "God's deed" to "human need" is often identified with René Descartes whose search for certainty led him to the famous insistence, "I think, therefore I am." Not only is the focus of this comment on the indubitable fact that a thinking being thinks, but Descartes constructs his entire philosophy on his certainty about himself as a thinking being. The result of Descartes's conviction was that everyone was encouraged to begin with the certainty of his or her own existence and then to think outward toward all other realities. Obviously, some distinction between God and one's self existed before Descartes, but Descartes turned the distinction into a division. The idea of a separate self, with no necessary relation to God and the world, may at least be said to begin with him.

The connection to God remains in the minds of many people entirely a matter of personal choice. While the reality of sin separates us from God, God's love for us initiates a new relationship with us while we are still sinners (Rom. 5:8). Thus, we can put too strong an emphasis on the act of our choosing God, as though we were the major actors in the drama of salvation. Scripture, however, teaches that we do not choose God. Rather God chooses us (John 15:16). Of course, God's dealing with us is a great mystery, and no one wants to deny our personal responsibility to God and each other. But we need to recognize that the credit for faith belongs to God and not to us. Faith that is recognized as a divine gift rather than a human achievement rests confidently in God rather than anxiously upon the self.

The Apostle Paul tells us "by grace you have been saved through faith; and this is not your own doing, it is the gift of God—not because of works, lest any man should boast." (Eph. 2:8–9) Thus, faith is defined as the gift that is an expression of God's love revealed in Jesus Christ, established at God's initiative by the special work of the Holy Spirit who joins us to Jesus Christ, and involving our trust in God's gift rather than confidence in our choices. This message needs to be heard again today, and perhaps most especially in North America because of our strong tendencies to think that we can in all matters, even spiritual matters, pull ourselves up by our own bootstraps and that faith is a matter of private will and decision. While most Protestant Christians accept salvation by God's grace alone through faith alone, some do not notice the admonition that this is not our own doing but a gift of God. Faith expresses the chief mystery of God's dealing with us, and therefore no final definition of faith is possible from the human side because faith as a gift is a divine action. That is, faith in God is not a matter of our nature but of God's grace. Therefore the credit for faith belongs to God and not us. Faith is not a work we produce by our own effort.

Unfortunately we hear too much today about "my" faith or "our" faith as if it were a personal possession. Likewise, the recommendation that we have or need greater faith assumes a process over which a person has if not total, then very considerable, control. In opposition to this view, faith in God describes both a relationship and an initiative. In faith the initiative belongs to God. Faith is a gift that in being bestowed makes us free to respond to God. God is thus both the object of human faith and the subject who bestows faith upon us. We are not passive and uninvolved in faith, but in considering faith we should praise God's grace rather than credit ourselves for the relationship.

Two misunderstandings about faith require special attention. First is the widespread confusion over the relation of faith and works, to which we have already briefly referred. The second is the difference between general and special grace.

Faith and Works

The fierce debate over the relationship of faith and works goes back to the Protestant Reformation of the sixteenth century. Roman Catholics insisted that one is saved by God's grace through faith *and* works. Faith is God's gift, but this gift is understood as reciprocally related to works or human actions. In this view, a person is saved not by the operation of the divine gift of faith alone but also by the human cooperation of obedience. Thus, to Roman Catholics salvation includes a component of human choice and effort.

Another sixteenth-century group, the radical reformers (and today's modern holiness groups), teach that people are saved by God's grace through faith for holy works. They claim human beings have three births: creation, justification, and sanctification. The Christian life leads through being declared righteous by faith in Jesus Christ to the actuality of the holy life. That is, the fullness of the holy life is something both attainable and expected. This view is open to criticism for denying the terrible reality of sin that still abides in the faithful. John Calvin, for one, insisted that as long as we are on earth we remain sinful and that to imagine we could ever reach human perfection (holiness) on earth is a great sin of arrogance. We note in passing that Presbyterians and United Methodists are still divided on this issue.

Calvin and Martin Luther taught that we are saved by God's grace through faith *alone*. However, they did not intend to divorce faith from works since they were aware that "faith by itself, if it has not works, is dead." (James 2:17) A better way to state their view is that "Salvation (or justification) comes by God's grace through faith alone *but not without works*," or that faith as God's gift completes our salvation. The Roman Catholic view sees faith and obedience (works) in a circular rather than sequential relationship. The Protestant view, on the other hand, is "linear" in that faith (as God's gift) comes first and work (as a human effort) accompanies and is a response to the gift of faith. This sequential pattern is also present in the relation between justification and sanctification (as we shall see in chapters 7 and 9). Calvin calls justification and sanctification "twin graces," but they are not identical twins. Justification is God's once-and-for-all forgiveness of our sin that is revealed in Jesus Christ. Sanctification, which follows justification, is our every day striving, with the aid of the Holy Spirit, to live a more holy life.

A problem developed among Protestants, however, when they tried to answer the question, "Am I saved?" On the one hand, they believed that salvation came by faith alone, but on the other they found faith was impossible to measure. A solution was proposed in what was called "the practical syllogism." The practical syllogism accepts that one cannot calculate salvation directly. However since works always follow faith and one can identify the fruits of the Spirit, deducing from one's works the strength of the faith that inspired them is possible. Nevertheless, in spite of the understandable desire to establish the certainty of salvation (see chapter 15), this view places an erroneous focus on human effort rather than the praise of divine grace. Since faith is a gift of God we can (and must) accept it with gratitude, but we cannot demand it.

In summary, the traditional Protestant view holds that salvation comes by God's grace through faith alone but not without works. Faith leads to works (the fruits of faith), and the presence of works demonstrates the existence of faith. However, works are not the *condition* of salvation but the *consequence* of it. This point is very important. God's salvation leads us to purity of life, but our purity of life does not produce salvation. We may be encouraged when we consider our efforts to serve God, but we may not place our confidence in these efforts. Works are neither the foundation of our salvation nor the ground of our recognition of it. Works are not the "cause" but the "because": works are not the expected *cause* of salvation, but rather *because* of salvation works are expected.

Universal and Special Grace

A second major problem concerned with the mystery of faith involves the proper understanding of grace. If both faith and grace are gifts of God, as orthodox Christianity has always maintained, why do some people receive these gifts and others not? This question is not an abstraction, but an honest query that can burn in our hearts and cause much distress. Many of us have raised this question with regard to family members and close friends. Sometimes we wonder about our own relation to grace and faith. We know that faith is the result of the loving will of God revealed in our Lord, Jesus Christ, but still we struggle with the relation of faith and election (predestination), human freedom, and God's providence. In this connection, many theologians, especially in the Reformed theological tradition, address the issue by making a distinction between (1) God's general or common grace universally bestowed on the world, and (2) God's special grace bestowed on individuals.

One of the main purposes of making these distinctions is to justify the mystery of faith as the bestowal of God's gift. Because obviously not everyone believes Jesus Christ is Lord (Phil. 2:11), the notion of common grace allows Christians to confess that God loves and nurtures all his human creatures. Special grace allows Christians to acknowledge that God chooses to *save* some of his human creatures. Each confession is true and necessary.

A problem arises because the relation between general and special grace is not resolved simply. The Bible uses both inclusive (the "alls") and exclusive (the "somes") language. For example, according to 1 Timothy 2:4, God desires all peoples to be saved. Matthew 22:14 teaches that many are called but only some are chosen. People who emphasize the "all" aspect can be attacked as "universalists" who deny the enormity of sin. Others who emphasize the "some" aspect can be attacked as limiting atonement and denying the magnitude of God's grace and love. The result of the distinction between common and special grace really only delays (and perhaps hides) the issue of faith's mystery, for no matter how much the blessings of general grace are praised, faith is not a general but a special grace.

Faith is God's special gift in that it does not happen "above us" or "below us" but "to us" and "in us" and "with us." Faith in the God revealed in Jesus Christ does not simply happen *above* us as a heavenly action regardless of our involvement. Yet asserting our lack of merit in receiving the gift of faith is important, primarily because faith comes to us as a blessing or as a gift that we are not owed and cannot earn. Likewise, faith does not simply happen *below* us as an event in the personal or collective subconscious that catches us unaware. Nevertheless, we must recognize that our lives are often deeply influenced by persons and events apart from our deliberate choices. Faith is a gift of God, bestowed at God's initiative and within the context of God's love. Faith involves not less than our response to God but a great deal more. This relationship is the heart of the mystery of faith.

In summary, the mystery of faith is great. Nevertheless, the real credit for faith belongs to God's love and not to our choice. Thinking of ourselves as separate from God and believing that our task is to find God through faith understood as a human work is a great temptation—especially in evangelical circles in North America. Nevertheless, while we are obviously involved, responsible, and accountable for our lives, we are neither the creators nor redeemers of them. Christians need to reemphasize that faith is a gift of God and to realize that we receive this gift already standing within God's grace. John Calvin put it simply and clearly when he noted that "faith is the principal work of the Holy Spirit." (*Inst.* III.1.4)

Union with Christ

To understand faith in a fully Christian way we must introduce a topic that will arise again in many of the following chapters: our union with Christ. Faith, as we have seen, is a gift of God's love given in Jesus Christ, which involves our trust in God's gift rather than confidence in our choices. This gift of faith has a special characteristic that marks it as Christian: Faith is established at God's initiative by the special work of the Holy Spirit who joins us to Jesus Christ, to share in His communion with and mission from the Father.[1]

Faith is being united to Christ by the Holy Spirit and, in relationship with him, sharing in his continuing life of adoration, obedience, and love. In union with Christ, that which is his becomes ours. His Father becomes our Father. His knowledge and love and service of the Father become, in union with him, our knowledge and love and service of our Father. In other words, Jesus Christ and our union with him through the Holy Spirit determine Christian faith, so much so that our union with Christ is the proper framework within which we understand the meaning of Christian faith in all regards. The apostle Paul teaches about faith in verses like: "In him we live and move and have our being" (Acts 17:28), and "Your life is hid with Christ in God."

(Col. 3:3)

The context for understanding the gift of faith, and everything else for that matter, is the doctrine of our union with Christ, which is the central, organizing feature of all Christian faith and life. Therefore the doctrine of our union with Christ is a basic belief that influences every other belief. In all things we do not stand before God on the strength of our own piety, faith, good works, and the like. Rather, because the Holy Spirit joins us to Jesus Christ we share in everything that is his. In and through him we are children of the heavenly Father, sharing in his own life in and before and from God. Joined to Jesus Christ we share in the communion and mission of the Holy Trinity. We stand before God in his name alone. And we serve in his name alone. The real meaning of the Christian's faith is the trust that *for Christ's sake* we are enfolded into the inner life of the Holy Trinity, to share in our Lord's communion with the Father and in his mission from the Father.

This view of faith explains the meaning of our baptism. We are baptized *into* the name of the Father, the Son, and the Holy Spirit. Thus in God we live and move and have our being. Because we are united with Christ, for example, he takes our sin as his own and bestows his obedience upon us. Calvin writes, "For this reason, he is called 'our Head' [Ephesians 4:15] and 'the first-born among many brethren' [Rom. 8:29]. We also, in turn, are said to be 'engrafted into him' [Rom. 11:17], and to 'put on Christ' [Gal. 3:27]; for as I have said, all that he possesses is nothing to us until we grow into one body with him." (*Inst.* III.1.1)

If Christ remains outside of us we do not receive the benefits of his work. We must, therefore, be joined to him, and in such a way that he defines our life. "For to me, living is Christ," Paul writes. (Phil. 1.21) This union applies both to the objective work of salvation, our being forgiven, and to our personal transformation from sinners into saints, our regeneration and sanctification. It is God who not only justifies, but also who sanctifies (1 Cor. 1:30). Necessarily, then, a double grace exists, for Christ's work has two dimensions in this regard. Says Calvin: "By partaking of him, we principally receive a double grace: namely, that being reconciled to God through Christ's blamelessness, we may have in heaven instead of a judge a gracious Father; and sec-ondly, that sanctified by Christ's Spirit we may cultivate blamelessness and purity of life." (*Inst.* III.11.1)

At the beginning of his discussion of faith and the Christian life in Book III of the *Institutes*, Calvin asks how the things that Christ has accomplished come to have any relevance for us. Calvin maintains,

> First, we must understand that as long as Christ remains out-side of us, and we are separated from him, all that he has suf-fered and done for the salvation of the human race remains useless and of no value for us. Therefore, to share with us what he has received from the Father, he had to become ours and dwell within us. (*Inst.* III.1.1)

In other words, for Christ's work to benefit us we must be united with him and he with us. Thus, according to Calvin,

> That joining together of Head and members, that indwelling of Christ in our hearts—in short, that mystical union—are accorded by us the highest degree of importance, so that Christ, having been made ours, makes us sharers with him in the gifts with which he has been endowed. We do not, there-fore, contemplate him outside ourselves from afar in order that his righteousness may be imputed to us but because we put on Christ and are engrafted into his body—in short because he deigns to make us one with him. (*Inst.* III.11.10)

This union of the believer with Christ and of Christ with us is the principal work of the Holy Spirit.

In his commentary on 1 Corinthians, Calvin notes "that it is only after we possess Christ himself that we share in the benefits of Christ. And I further maintain that he is possessed not only when we believe that he was sacrificed for us, but when he dwells in us, when he is one with us, when we are members of his flesh, in short, when we become united in one life and substance, in a manner of speaking, with him."[2] Calvin's commentary identifies the great evangelical doctrine of our union with Christ on which the whole of the Christian life depends.

Bound to Christ through the bond of the Holy Spirit, we receive his benefits, and in receiving his benefits, his righteousness and holi-ness become our righteousness and holiness. This work of God makes both salvation and the Christian life possible. Says Calvin: "When we hear mention of our union with God, let us remember that holiness must be its bond; not because we come into communion with him by virtue of our holiness! Rather, we ought to cleave unto him so that, infused with his holiness, we may follow whither he calls." (*Inst.* III.11.2)

In this doctrine of Christ's union with us and of our union with Christ in the power of the Spirit, we find the thread that ties together our confession of Christ with our understanding of faith, discipleship, authority, mission, and Church unity. As the Holy Spirit unites believers with Jesus Christ, our faith and discipleship become an expression and an outgrowth of his life within us: "It is no longer I who live, but Christ who lives in me." (Gal. 2:20) Our approach to Scripture finds its anchor in Christ's own knowledge of the Father: "'For who has known the mind of the Lord so as to instruct him?' But we have the mind of Christ." (1 Cor. 2:16) Our mission becomes a participation in and extension of his mission from the Father for the sake of the world: "As the Father has sent me, even so I send you." (John 20:21) Our unity with one another emerges as the product of our union with him: "So we, though many, are one body in Christ, and individually members one of another." (Rom. 12:5)

Perhaps the most touching, winsome, and poignant statement John Calvin ever wrote is this: "Take courage, my friends. Even if we are nothing in our own hearts, perchance something of us is safely hidden in the heart of God." (*Inst.* III.2.25) Calvin is here reflecting Colossians 3:3, which affirms that our "life is hid with Christ in God." According to Karl Barth, the twentieth-century Reformed theologian, this verse is the center of the gospel.[3]

In any case, the mystery of faith is the principal work of the Holy Spirit, who is the bond of union between the Father and Son and the bond between the divine being and the human being. Faith is the confidence that because we are united with Jesus Christ, all that is his has become ours, and all that is ours—broken and feeble as it most likely is—is now also his, and in him healed and made holy before God. This healing is the fruit of the "wonderful exchange." (*Inst.* IV.17.2) on which everything turns and that gives Christian faith and the Christian's faith their identifying marks.

3

The Fatherhood of God

As a student I had a dear friend, an Orthodox Jew, who taught Hebrew in a synagogue in Edinburgh and was both well informed about his faith and feisty in its defense. I was quite new to Christian faith and aggressive about some matters of doctrine that I really knew little about. My friend enjoyed poking holes in my blustery arguments, although always with good humor and gentle grace. One day, as we walked home from a Jewish-Christian dialogue meeting hosted by a local political association (we were members of the same political party) he turned to me and said, "You know, your Christianity is just an accident of birth. If you were born somewhere else you would have a different religion. By what name would you call God then?" Chapters 3, 4, and 5, give an account of the Christian doctrine of God as the Father, the Son, and the Holy Spirit, one God, Holy Trinity. Perhaps now, many years later, a more adequate reply to his question can be provided.

The question of the identity of God goes back to the beginning of Israel's story. Exodus 3 contains the account of Moses being confronted by God out of the burning bush, and of God giving him his charge to lead the Israelites out of bondage in Egypt. Moses responded, "If I come to the Israelites and say to them, 'The God of your ancestors has sent me to you,' and they ask me, 'What is his name?' what shall I say to them?" (3:13) The answer for both Moses and Israel is given in the divine name. "God said to Moses, 'I AM WHO

I AM.' (3:14) The name of the Lord is not arbitrary. It is God-given. It is revealed. We do not make up the name of God.

In the New Testament Jesus reveals in a yet fuller way the name of God. John 1:18 is an important verse in this regard. "No one has ever seen God. It is God the only Son, who is close to the Father's heart, who has made him known." Two points should be noted. First, Jesus reveals God because he is God. Second, as Son of God, he makes known or interprets God as the Father. He does not, then, reveal something about God, but takes us into the reality of God in such a way that he reveals "the personal Name of God in which the form and content of this self-revelation as Father through Jesus Christ his Son are inseparable."[1]

The doctrine of God is presented in the traditional order, Father, Son, and Holy Spirit, because it is familiar, although Jesus Christ is the Son of God who reveals the Father, and to whom the Holy Spirit bears witness. Further, while Christian tradition has insisted that a time never existed when the Son was not, and that the Father is Father precisely as Father of the Son, a sense is also present in which the Father is the eternal Creator and Lord, as the Nicene Creed makes clear.

A Contested Doctrine

For this discussion, beginning with a strong statement on the Christian doctrine of the Fatherhood of God would make sense. However, the doctrine of the Fatherhood of God has been a serious point of contention for some time now in North American Protestantism. On the one hand, Jesus taught us to pray, "Our Father, who art in heaven," and Christian tradition names God as One Being, Three Persons, the Father, the Son and the Holy Spirit. The doctrine of the Fatherhood of God is the church's way of speaking about our participation in Jesus Christ's own relationship with, and especially his prayer to, the One whom he knew as Father. Feminist critics, on the other hand, argue that the use of the term "father" for God, while not wrong as such, has been elevated into such a singular position that other words of address to God have been neglected, patriarchalism is ratified, and women's experience is excluded from Christian expression. Because we are reflecting here on one of the greatest of all the-

ological mysteries—namely, how do we speak of and address God—
these questions will take us into complex matters that are close to the
center of Christian faith and life itself.

A dear friend and a faithful colleague in ministry brought these
concerns home to me when she explained her difficulty with the
Lord's Prayer. She is traditional in theology, especially with regard to
the person and work of Jesus Christ. Although she holds to the doctrine of the Trinity in a formal way, she finds the doctrine of the
Fatherhood of God as a faithful expression of Christian teaching hard
to deal with on a personal level. The issue for her is that relating to
God as "Father" remains especially difficult because of the patriarchy
in Christian tradition and her personal history with her biological
father, a man of stern authority and emotional remoteness. In such a
circumstance, while prayer to "Our Father" can make sense to her
intellectually, it carries such a burden of social, religious, and personal
history that praying in a relational way to God as Father is still
uncomfortable on an emotional level.

Long ago, Christian teachers spoke about Christian truth descend-
ing from the mind into the heart. Just understanding doctrine, and
getting the words and arguments right, is not enough. We must also
come to love the God to whom doctrine refers. Mouthing correct
doctrine without a lively relationship with God is not an adequate
expression of Christian experience. We must do more than give an
account of the meaning of the Fatherhood of God, no matter how
convincing, and we must have an awareness of the very serious and
real problems that such language raises for some people, both men
and women.

The theological challenge that is put to the traditional Trinitarian
naming of God as the Father, the Son, and the Holy Spirit, One God,
focuses on the dominance of this one name for God: Father. Over and
against the use of the Fatherhood of God, feminist critics often prefer
the metaphor of the reign of God as the imaginative religious basis for
human liberation. The concern is patriarchalism, and the argument is
made that if God is male, then the male is in the image of the divine
and in charge. Identifying God as the Father ratifies an ordered, top-
down understanding of the cosmos that forms the basis for the orders
of creation in which men exercise lordship over women. Because only
men model God (God is Father and not Mother), women are not

'named' by God. Men, in this case, have a role model in God that women do not. Critics charge that the root metaphor of the Fatherhood of God, then, operates as a code for a religious ordering of the world in which women are always inferior to men because the world is interpreted "patriarchally."

Feminist critics argue that Jesus did not endorse patriarchalism, but advanced an alternative, namely the reign or rule of God as the arena for the liberation of women and men from divinely sanctioned role models that left women subject to men. Characteristic of this alternative view is giving attention to relationship with God as friend rather than to descriptions of God as Father. In this case, appeal is made to John 15:14–15, for example: "You are my friends if you do what I command you. I do not call you servants (Gk. 'slave') any longer." In the reign of God both men and women have relationships of mutuality and equality, all ministries of the church are open to both, and relationship with God is one of loving a friend in faithfulness rather than obedience to a master.

Clearly the issue is much more than, although it includes, women's rights. The debate is over the specifically Christian apprehension of God. That men have used religious language to justify the subjugation of woman is beyond dispute. The feminist critique helps us to recognize the misuse of theology for misogynist ends, for such a viewpoint points to alternative practical models for understanding and living Christian faith that are both faithful to the gospel and morally superior to hierarchical and patriarchal relations.

However, certain questions must be asked of these people who criticize the traditional naming of God as Father. The insight that the reign of God has to do with relationships is correct, but the heart of the New Testament is not the *reign* of God, but the reign of *God*. In other words, the subject of the Gospel is not reign but God, specifically that Christians must confess the relationship between the Father and the Son in the power of the Holy Spirit because that is who God is revealed to be in the New Testament. The problem with feminist theology at this point is its avoidance of naming God on a specifically Christian basis. An attempt to advance a Christian theology that eschews the Fatherhood of God eschews also the doctrine of the Trinity, and surrenders thereby the doctrine of the Sonship of Jesus Christ as Son of the Father. This flaw is fatal, for such a theology is no longer a Christian doctrine of God, or a theology of a God who saves, or a theology of relationship with God. We can hardly be in a relationship with God apart from knowing *who* God is, and apart from God's given way of our being in that relationship. Avoiding the Father-Son relationship means denying the way in which God has elected to disclose himself and bring us into relationship with himself. In the deliberate avoidance of the doctrines of the Trinity as the Father, the Son, and the Holy Spirit, one God, and the vicarious priesthood of Jesus Christ by whom and through whom we come to the Father, God remains unknown and unloved. How ironic that the relational theology that feminists so rightly desire is in fact the fruit of the doctrine of the Holy Trinity, the Father, the Son, and the Holy Spirit, one God, the very approach to God that they reject.

The Christian Doctrine of the Fatherhood of God

1. We know God as Father because Jesus, the Son of God, reveals God as his Father. As indicated briefly earlier, the Christian doctrine of the Fatherhood of God is deeply bound up with the revelation of Jesus Christ as God's beloved Son. Knowledge of the Father and the Son are profoundly connected in such a way that our knowledge of the Father is in and through His revelation of the Son as his Son. "Who do you say that I am?" (Mark 8:27–30) Jesus' question at Caesarea Philippi, then as now, is the central question. Functionally, the Christian doctrine of God stands or falls on the answer. Further, the doctrine of the Fatherhood of God stands or falls on the ground of the doctrine of the Trinity. If Jesus is not the Son of the Father, but is instead a religious man who just called God "Father" because God is like a father, the doctrines of the Trinity and of the Fatherhood of God are arguably best forgotten for they have then no basis in God. If Jesus were merely human, providing an instance of religious experience, acting as a symbol or pointer to a God who otherwise remains hidden, then the doctrine of the Trinity is indeed an appendix to Christian theology.[2] The doctrine of the Fatherhood of God in that case has no anchor in God's self-revelation and is, as feminist critics argue, replaceable, for reasons already noted.

But to the contrary, the doctrines of the Trinity and the Fatherhood of God were impressed upon the mind of the Church in large part because Christians were compelled to deal with who Jesus was as living Lord and beloved Son of the Father. In Jesus, the incarnation of the Word of God, God really was seen to have entered into our human experience in two ways. First, because Jesus was fully God, our salvation in Christ and our knowledge of God are rooted in God. Second, because Jesus was fully human, salvation and knowledge of God take form within Jesus' human experience in history as a life lived before God. The Church's experience of Jesus as Lord, both as God and as a man, led to the huge leap of theological imagination in which a profound connection was made between the act and identity of God in Jesus. In fact, it entailed a revolution in talk about God. Specifically Christian talk about God as the Father, the Son, and the Holy Spirit was seen, not only to be made possible, but also to be compelled, by the Church's experience of Jesus as Lord.

One way to understand how this arose is to inquire about the Christian experience of Holy Communion. At the Lord's Supper, do Christians merely recall an ancient story? Or is the living Lord really present in the broken bread and poured-out wine? In the elements of bread and wine do we truly receive the body and blood of Jesus Christ, and through this communion with Christ enter into communion with the Father? And even more: Are we present also with the host of heaven in this communion with Jesus Christ?

At the heart of our salvation, and the basis for a specifically Christian doctrine of God, is the twofold nature of the ministry of Christ. Take, for example, Hebrews 3:1: Jesus is referred to as "the apostle and high priest of our confession." What does this mean? First, in Jesus' incarnation and atonement he comes as the true apostle of God. He reveals to us the love of the Father as he bears the cost of our sins. He comes not just to tell us about God, but as God he reveals and acts out in his very personhood the will of the Father. Second, as our High Priest, he is also the word and act of humankind to the Father, offering the life of worship, prayer, and obedience that God requires. He not only bears our separation from God vicariously, but he also stands in for us as the One who as God in the flesh offers to God the truly human life. The grace of the gospel does not end with the 'descent,' as it were, of God to us in Christ, but includes the 'ascent' of Jesus in his human life of filial obedience and love before the Father. This two-way relationship between the Father and the Son in the power of the Holy Spirit is the center of the New Testament.

In the Spirit (for more discussion see chapter 5) Jesus Christ, risen and reigning, joins us to his relationship of filial love by adoption, through our union with him, teaching us, when we pray, to say, "Our Father." The atonement is properly understood to include both the death of Jesus in our stead on the cross *and* the at-one-ment of communion between God and humankind in himself. This relationship is the inner core of Christian truth and experience. Explained in this way, the doctrine of our salvation clearly includes the doctrine of the person and work of Christ and the doctrine of the Trinity. Understanding who Jesus is, as the ground for understanding his work, forces a specifically Trinitarian understanding of God upon the Christian mind.

2. The second aspect of the Christian doctrine is the naming of the Trinitarian God. But what about alternative names for the Persons of the Trinity? The naming of the Trinitarian God as the Father, the Son, and the Holy Spirit is frequently replaced today by the supposed functional equivalent of Creator, Redeemer, and Sustainer—in truth, parts of God's "job description." Obviously, the issue involves the reality of God and the nature and ground of theological language about God.

How does human language work in reference to a divine subject? The language we use in theology is the language of ordinary speech taken from common experience. The theology we do is done in Pittsburgh. One of us thinks in a Scottish accent, the other in an American accent. Similarly, the doctrine of the Trinity arose out of centuries of reflection by the people of God seeking to understand scripture and their experience of the living Lord Jesus in their actual historical contexts. However, the meaning we give to words in ordinary experience is not necessarily the meaning they have in theology.

The Reformed tradition teaches that we speak of God by the mouth of Jesus, meaning that while using ordinary language, theological speech about God is filled from beyond itself with content that is given by God. This consequence of the doctrine of revelation and the authority of scripture is the critical point, and its effect is principally twofold. First, theological speech is speech that really does talk of God, but always in the language of human experience. Second, theological speech in its realism profoundly calls into question and dethrones all idols of the mind that we seek to project onto God. While we indeed speak about God, God is not reducible to these words. Even the most revered doctrinal language used by Christians is, at its most faithful, only a pointer to God and is not to be confused with God. Thus we speak of the *doctrine* of the Trinity. While the doctrine refers appropriately to God, and indeed protects the mystery of God, we do not confuse the doctrine with the reality of God. The doctrine is necessary and crucial, but the doctrine is not God.

However the Church has misused its language for God, we must try to understand what Christians traditionally have intended in their talk of the Fatherhood of God. Theologically, the reciprocal concepts of the Fatherhood of God and the Sonship of Jesus derive neither from an inherent likeness between the creature and the Creator, nor from a view of religious language that projects social and family values or political ideology onto God.[3] In speaking of the Fatherhood of God we are employing a human way of speaking about God, for we have no other way to speak. But neither the formative Greek-speaking Trinitarian theologians of the fourth century, nor the Reformers of the sixteenth, thought when they spoke of the Fatherhood of God that they were projecting human values and aspiration onto God. Rather, they believed that God was revealed in, by, and through Jesus, and thus could speak of God by the mouth of Jesus. A number of biblical texts lay behind their kind of thinking:

> Whoever has seen me has seen the Father. (John 14:9)
> No one knows the Son except the Father, and no one knows the Father except the Son *and anyone to whom the Son chooses to reveal him*. (Matt. 11:27, emphasis added)
> No one has ever seen God. It is God the only Son, who is close to the Father's heart, *who has made him known*. (John 1:18, emphasis added)

The son interprets the Father, to translate the literal meaning of the last phrase of John 1:18. As noted repeatedly, of central importance for classical theology was the primacy of the Father-Son relationship.

In and through Jesus Christ we know God and can speak about God in a faithful way, as when the writer of the Epistle to the Ephesians states that, "In [Jesus Christ] we have access to God. . . . For this reason I bow my knees before the Father, from whom every family in heaven and on earth takes its name." (Eph. 3:12, 14–15) For this same reason, further, Christian theological tradition teaches that our speech concerning the Fatherhood of God is controlled by God's self-revelation in Jesus Christ. Rejected is the view that theological language is the projection of ourselves onto God, making the human male the basis of our language for God.

The concept of God's Fatherhood is tied utterly to Jesus' naming of his own relationship to the Father, into which relationship we by the Spirit participate through our union with Christ. The Father is the Father of our Lord Jesus Christ. Whenever 'Father' is used of God in the classical tradition the word always means 'the one whom Jesus called Father and knew as Father.' The term does not denote a generic title for God outside of the Father-Son relationship. God's Fatherhood was understood in terms of God's relationship with and revealed act in Jesus Christ, and not as a human image or concept projected onto God. Theological talk of God had its transcendent ground in Jesus' relationship with the One whom he called 'Abba,' which had nothing to do whatsoever with general male experiences of fatherhood.

In fact we must necessarily avoid assigning any biological or sexual imputation whatsoever into the theological concept of God. God the Father revealed in Christ and attested in scripture has no sexual identity. Sexuality, after all, is part of creation, as Genesis 1 and 2 make clear. In any case, using creation as the content for speech about God would be idolatry. The image of God is not reversible! It goes in one direction only.

The personalized language of Trinitarian theology intended to bear witness in Christ, and especially in the cross, to the liberation of humankind from all patriarchal idols and divinized ideologies. Where the male is worshipped and glorified in and through theological reference to the Fatherhood of God is a perversion that must be criticized on the ground of the Christian doctrine of God itself. The great danger in losing Trinitarian language for God and replacing it with either an apparently gender-neutral functional language or with some reimagined language is that we lose reference to God, the Father, the Son, and the Holy Spirit.

By the mouth of Christ we call God 'Our Father.' But note that we do not speak this in words only. For above all the goal of our salvation, of which now we have a foretaste, through our union with Christ is to share in a relationship, the communion of love between the Father and the Son in the power of the Spirit. Only in and through the Sonship of Jesus do we know the Fatherliness of the Father and can pray "Our Father, who art in heaven." In Christ and from Christ we inherit the Father as our Father. The gift of the Father to us in and through Jesus Christ is the gift of sharing in the communion of the Son with the Father. Christ shows that the love with which the Father loves him and he loves the Father is for us and in us through himself as we are joined to him through the bond of the Holy Spirit. In and through Jesus Christ we come not only to know God as the Father, and to speak thus, but also to live with God as our Father, who loves us from eternity and brings us home through his beloved Son. We come to know ourselves as dear children of the almighty Father, by adoption through Christ.

Praying "Our Father, who art in heaven . . ." really means that apart from Christ we are orphans, lost and homeless. However, he has not only revealed that God is a God of love, but also that God is our Father by the grace of our sharing in his own unique Sonship through the bond of the Holy Spirit.

Clearly Trinitarian doctrine has profound implications for the frame of reference within which we live our lives. By baptism we are enfolded into the communion of love that characterizes the life of the Trinity. In worship, we who are joined to Christ by our baptism share in his eternal adoration of and love for the Father. In prayer, what is his by nature becomes ours by grace as we share in his intimate fellowship with the Father. Everything else in Christian faith and life flows from this sharing. For these reasons, Christianity claims the Fatherhood of God, understood in the light of the ministry of Jesus Christ, as an integral aspect of the full doctrine of God's grace.

4

The Lordship of Christ

Not long after beginning my second pastorate I went for a haircut at the local barbershop. When my turn came and I settled into the chair, the friendly barber said, "I haven't seen you before. Are you new in town?"

"Yes," I said. "I've been here a week."

The conversation, I assumed, would then move on to safe topics like the weather or sports. However, he had the curiosity of a small-town barber, so the next question was, "What do you do in town?"

"I'm the new pastor at the church around the corner."

"Well," he replied, "That's nice. I am not religious myself."

"Neither am I," was my reply.

At this point things grew very quiet. How could I be a pastor and not religious? What kind of game was this guy playing? And I realized then that it's not smart to mess around with the mind of a man who is standing behind you with a straight razor in his hand.

Many people think that being Christian and being religious are the same thing. According to them religion is the general category and Christianity is a specific example of it. This outlook would be accurate if religion were correctly defined as the human effort to encounter God and Christianity were understood as one of the possible manifestations of that quest, a particular illustration of the genus "religion." At many levels Christianity does look and act like a religion, but in its essential reality the Christian faith is *not* a human effort to encounter God. Rather the Christian faith is the result of God's effort revealed in Jesus Christ to encounter the human. We dealt with that approach in a personal way in chapter 1. In this chapter we turn to the central subject of Christian faith, Jesus Christ, the One in and through whom God savingly encounters us, and by whom we have communion with the Father.

Surely, one would think, whatever else Christianity might affirm, the most central and incontrovertible doctrine must be the doctrine of Christ as Lord and Savior. After all, the apostle Paul teaches that if we confess with our lips that Jesus Christ is Lord, and believe in our hearts that God raised him from the dead, we will be saved (Rom. 10:10). Apart from Jesus Christ how could there be any Christianity at all? Of course, we can and do debate what Christology—the doctrine of Jesus Christ—means precisely. Various legitimate informed understandings exist of our Lord's person and work. But surely a sophisticated denial of Jesus Christ as the Lord of the entire created order would not seem to be a Christian option.

However, in our time once again the question is raised with great urgency, "Who is Jesus Christ?" Each generation and each person must answer that question directly and individually. Because the question is so crucial and the topic so complex, many answers have been given over the centuries. We cannot even attempt to outline the historical and theological development of the doctrine of Christ in any detail, but we can summarize.

Two major Christological eras have occurred, two times of the church in which the doctrine of Christ was debated with special clarity and importance. The first extended from the ministry of Jesus through the Nicene Creed (325) and the Chalcedonian Formula (451). The conclusion was that Jesus Christ is really and fully God and really and fully man.[1] This agreement was generally maintained through the Middle Ages, the Reformation, and early modern history. The second era began around 1800 (with philosopher Immanuel Kant) and is still developing today. In this view Jesus Christ is not God and a man, representing all people—one person in two natures—but a symbol or ideal or example of the proper relation between God and humankind.

We regard this development with considerable alarm because Christians are always tempted to accommodate themselves to the views of the secular culture that surrounds them. We believe this modern reinterpretation of the Lordship of Christ must be mightily resisted. It does not represent the teaching of the Bible or the Christian tradition or even the present mind of the church in all of its main denominations. It represents *avant garde* theorizing. In a general way since Kant, many people have believed that the heart of religion is ethics and the church should foster Christian love in personal relationships and society and forget about Christian doctrine. Jesus, they think, was really a teacher of ethics and not a savior of sinners and the One in and through whom we have communion with the Father. This line of thinking has led in recent theology to a shift from the orthodox and creedal view that God is revealed *in* Jesus Christ to the "advanced" view that God is only revealed *by* Jesus Christ. We will not pursue this complicated issue except to repeat the conviction that the recent view of Jesus as human example only is quite wrong.

The next three sections contain a short sketch of the Lordship of Christ based on the biblical, historical, and theological witness. Then a brief discussion follows of the work of Christ by way of the traditional threefold office, and a conclusion.

Jesus Christ—Our Lord

The first certainty for the first Christians was that Jesus Christ was both their Lord and Savior and Lord of all. Each book of the New Testament testifies to this conviction in its own way. On nearly every page of the New Testament the person and work of Jesus Christ is discussed. An important instance of the affirmation of the Lordship of Jesus Christ is given in the Caesarea Philippi story. Caesarea Philippi figures only once in the gospel accounts, as the setting for the great "who" question that Jesus put to his disciples: "Who do people say that I am?" (Mark 8:27) Caesarea Philippi, now the modern area of Banyas, is nestled on the terraced slopes at the foot of Mount Hermon, at the northern end of what today is known as the Golan Heights. Two things are interesting about the place. Out of a huge open-faced cave in the rock flows one of the principal sources of the Jordan River. Also, the cave and the head of the river served as the site of three ancient pagan temples. Joshua 11:17 refers to a place called Baal-gad, below Mount Hermon, in the Valley of Lebanon. Baal-gad means "lord of fortune" and was likely the site of the Canaanite shrine now excavated at the cave mouth. In Greek times, after the conquest by Alexander the Great in 332 B.C., a temple was built on top of the old shrine to Pan and the Nymphs, and the district came to be known as Paneias. Then in Roman times, Herod built a marble temple there in honor of the Emperor Augustus, and he renamed the city Caesarea. Later the site became the headquarters of the Tetrarch Philip, son of Herod, mentioned at Luke 3:1, and became known as Philip's Caesarea, thus Caesarea Philippi, to distinguish it from the magnificent Mediterranean seaport of Caesarea.

Why is this important? To Jesus' question "Who do people say that I am?" we read the great declaration of Peter, "You are the Messiah, the Son of the Living God." (Matt. 16:16//Mark 8:27–29//Luke 9:18–20) The conversation, as noted above, happens in the context of and against the backdrop of three pagan temples. The question of the identity of Jesus as Lord is always a question that is discussed in the contexts of other claims to divinity. The affirmation of the Lordship of Jesus excludes other claims. The issue is who really is Lord? Is Jesus Christ Lord, or the gods of nature, of Greece, or of Rome, or today of America, of power, of money, or of our own ideological devising? Who do people say that the Son of Man is? That was Jesus' question to his disciples two thousand years ago. Our Lord puts that same question to us today, with many religions, many spiritualities, and many philosophies all claiming authority as the backdrop.

The affirmation "Jesus Christ is Lord" (Phil. 2:11) is the principal affirmation of the New Testament. In the Gospels, Jesus is frequently designated as Lord—in fact, more than one hundred times. The early church called on Jesus to forgive their sins; they worshipped him and declared him in the power of the Spirit *Jesous Kyrios*, Jesus Lord. In this way he was named with the holy name of God in the giving of the divine name to Israel.[2] For Paul and his tradition, this naming is the central claim. In sum, "if you confess with your lips that Jesus is Lord and believe in your heart that God raised him from the dead, you will be saved." (Rom. 10:9) The Lordship of Jesus Christ is affirmed in a number of notable passages (for example, at Col. 1:15–20 and Phil. 2:5–11). The theological interpretations of his birth, life, death, resurrection, and ascension found throughout the New Testament attest, both explicitly or implicitly, that Jesus is Lord.

For the post-resurrection church, the exaltation of Jesus increasingly made him the subject of worship. To be revered as teacher and healer was not enough. From the very beginning, the New Testament understood the Gospel story in the light of Jesus' cross, resurrection, and ascension. A way of thinking about Jesus was forced upon the mind of the church by the very subject matter of Christian faith itself, known in a living relationship with a living and reigning Lord. An understanding of Jesus separated from his Lordship—revealed in his cross, resurrection, and exaltation and known in the worship and the praying of the church—denies Jesus as Emmanuel, God with us in our flesh.

The great theological issue was how to hold together the central theistic affirmation, God is one (Deuteronomy 6), with the claim of the New Testament that Jesus is Lord. Thus began the Herculean process of thought in which the church had to think out the implications of its central affirmation. In other words, the staggering implication of the truth that Jesus is Lord, God as a man, meant inevitably a revolution in the doctrine of God in which a distinctly Christian doctrine of God had to be developed. Jesus was not just a man who revealed something about God—God revealed *by* Jesus. The events of his birth, life, and death, as well as his resurrection and ascension, had to be thought through not only insofar as they tell us about Jesus, but also insofar as they tell us from the inside, as it were, about God. In the person and work of Christ we deal directly with God—God revealed in Jesus. By the middle of the fourth century the meaning of the incarnation and atonement for the doctrine of God forced the church to develop the doctrine of the Trinity, which is the foundation of all Christian thinking.

Jesus Christ: One Person in Two Natures

One might think that the New Testament provides sufficient answers for all questions about the identity of Jesus Christ. However, that hope was forlorn because some Christians drew conclusions from scripture that others thought distorted its meaning. For example, the phrase "Son of God" was taken by some people to mean that Jesus was subordinate to God. Thus if Jesus was literally "God with us" ("Emmanuel"—Matt. 1:23) he would have been called God's "twin brother." In order to protect the mystery of Jesus as (a) the son of Mary who was (b) conceived by the Holy Spirit, the early church concluded and confessed that Jesus was both God and a man.

This answer to the identity of Jesus Christ—the Who and How question—produced a formula that raises as many questions as it answers, except that it has protected the reality of the mystery of God's revelation in Jesus Christ for nearly seventeen hundred years. As we have said, only in the last two hundred years have substitutions been recommended and only in the last forty years have alternatives been strongly urged.

To read back into the New Testament the magisterial creeds of Councils of Nicea (325) and Chalcedon (451)—which are the result of three and four hundred years of theological reflection on the New Testament, and the experience of faith in the risen and living Christ to which it bears witness—would be a serious error. The New Testament is not a textbook on theology from which truths can be deduced by logical inference. Rather the New Testament is the apostolic witness to Jesus Christ, a dynamic divine instrument given by the power of the Holy Spirit to bring knowledge of salvation to the world and to bring faith to men and women. Therefore, on the basis of its confession of Jesus Christ the New Testament forced the mind of the early church, as it were, to develop a historical doctrine that would protect the Biblical mystery. This doctrinal task was not easily accomplished. The debates were long, fierce, and extremely complicated. Quite obviously seventeen centuries cannot be adequately discussed in two paragraphs.

Nevertheless, a very simplified summary suggests the early church faced two issues: the "Who" question and the "How" question. That is, Who is this Jesus Christ, conceived by the Holy Spirit and born of Mary, that we confess as Lord? Some Christians, like Arius (d. 336), believed that Jesus was a wonderful man and very close (or similar) to God but he was not really God. His opponent, Athanasius (d. 373), known as the father of orthodoxy, insisted that our salvation was impossible if Jesus is only a human being. The "Who" question was resolved by the Nicene Creed (325) which taught that Jesus is of the same substance, or of one being (*homo-ousion*), with the Father, as Athanasius and many others believed, rather than of similar substance (*homoi-ousion*). The orthodox doctrine of the Lordship of Christ still rejects the small Greek letter, *iota*.

The "How" question naturally followed the "Who" question. That is to say, how are Christians supposed to understand that Jesus Christ is both God and a man? Three rejected views need a very brief discussion: To use percentages and to simplify greatly, the Apollinarians said Jesus is 60 percent divine and 40 percent human, which makes a 100 percent person. The Eutychians said Jesus was once human but his humanity was absorbed into his deity. The Nestorians thought Jesus remained 100 percent human and 100 percent divine but could not explain how Jesus could be one person with two complete (and completely different) natures. The Creed of Chalcedon (451) rejected Apollinarianism, Eutychianism, and Nestorianism and affirmed the "wise and saving creed" of Nicea. In addition Chalcedon taught that Our Lord Jesus Christ was "to be acknowledged in two natures, inconfusedly, unchangeably, indivisibly, inseparably." These terms were not explained, but the mystery of God's revelation in Jesus Christ—one person, two natures—was declared the orthodox belief of the Church.

Jesus Christ—The Same Today

The central affirmation of Christian faith that Jesus Christ is Lord is based on the biblical witness, understood and developed through many centuries of careful theological reflection on its mystery. This witness leads directly to the theological convictions that we assert in the face of modernist rejections.

The great declaration of Peter at Caesarea Philippi is again the critical issue in the church. The issue is whether some people are preaching and teaching another Christ (2 Cor. 11:4, and note the pastoral context of that verse). Once again the Christian church must decide whether the church believes the scriptural and confessional doctrine of the singular saving Lordship of Jesus Christ or whether the church believes only that he is one of many representatives of God—perhaps even the best, but not singularly savior and Lord. The latter view repeats the old Arian heresy, which is always a fundamental attack on the heart of the New Testament teaching and classical Christian doctrine. The Arian heresy and its contemporary versions deny the reality of Christ as Lord of *all*, as the final revelation of God, and as the only savior of the world. To put it clearly, orthodox Christians believe that Jesus is God, and not just a godly man. He is divine Savior and not merely a human religious genius. He is Redeemer and not only another teacher—albeit the most brilliant—of the moral way.

Recent enthusiasm for pluralism as a universal value has caused some Christians discomfort in making absolute claims concerning Jesus Christ for fear of excluding someone else's point of view and thereby delegitimating their experience. To hear Christians, and even Christian leaders, declare that Jesus is not *the* Lord, but *a* Lord, although *my* Lord, is not at all uncommon. This view holds that "Jesus is Lord of my life, but I have no right to proclaim that he is Lord of your life." Amid valid concerns for inclusivity in a pluralistic religious culture, this timidity about the most basic Christian claim means that some Christians have forgotten that the Church's one foundation is Jesus Christ her Lord. All around a profound spiritual hunger gives the Christian church an extraordinary evangelical opportunity, but too often the church's bugle plays uncertain and indistinct notes (1 Cor. 14:7–8). The church has lost confidence in its central message that not our experience, not even Scripture, but only Jesus is Lord. Jesus alone reveals God because he is really and fully God in the flesh of our humanity. Moreover, only Jesus saves us for he is really and fully a man who is God with and for us.

From the very beginning, and no less today, the core issue that focuses the mind of the Church is the understanding and proclamation of the Lordship of Jesus Christ. Every other issue in Christian doctrine, in practical faith, in ethics, and in ministry and mission, including our understanding of the authority and the nature of scripture, depends on our understanding and acceptance of the sole saving Lordship of Jesus, the only Son of the Father, who alone is the Way and the Truth and the Life.

Our Lord's Three Offices

Our discussion at this point can benefit from an examination of the concept of the Lordship of Christ and what it entails. As Lord, Jesus is the One who reconciles us to God, he is the word of God, and he rules in power in the name of God. In order to explain the relationship between who he is and what he does for us, Christian tradition has ascribed three offices to Jesus Christ—priest, prophet, and king—

intending to express in the unity of his person and work his identity and purpose as the Anointed One. The terms are functional and theological; they imply the person who bears them in a unity of work and person, act and being.

In the Old Testament these three figures were office-bearers of God.[3] The prophet spoke the word of God. The king reigned on earth on behalf of God. The priest interceded with God on behalf of the people. When the Christian tradition uses the threefold office of Christ, however, in view is not only continuity with Israel's prophets, priests, and kings, and the role they played, but also a profound discontinuity. In Christ these offices were not just fulfilled, but radically transformed. First, in Israel's experience the three figures were usually separate. In Christ they are held together in the unity of his person. Second, in Israel the three offices were often held in tension, and perhaps even in competition. The offices were not just taken over by the Church's doctrine of Jesus Christ, nor was this doctrine squeezed to fit into their shape. Rather, in Christ something new happened, as the old was redeployed in the service of the new reality in Jesus Christ.[4] In this way, Christ is as prophet, both Teacher and Teaching, as priest, both Priest and Sacrifice, and as king, both Victor and Victory,[5] in a way that profoundly redefines the terms in and through his own life and ministry.

As we have said throughout, to affirm that Jesus is Lord does not mean only that Jesus reveals God. As God and a man, as Lord in the flesh of our humanity, he is God with us *savingly* in this dual sense: through his union with us he saves us from our sins by bearing them in his own flesh *and* through our union with him he is the means of our living the Christian life before the Father. The Lordship of Jesus Christ means that in no one else are our sins forgiven, and through no one else are we restored to communion with the Father. For this reason the priestly office especially needs to be emphasized.

The priestly office of Jesus Christ is the heart of the doctrine of salvation and the cornerstone that carries the weight of the gospel. Christ's priesthood includes, first, the forgiving act of God dealing with us as sinners in the incarnate flesh of Jesus of Nazareth (about which we will say more in chapter 7). Second, the priesthood includes the human work of Jesus Christ in response in his dealing with the Father on our behalf, as our representative before God (which is the basis for the struggle for saintliness, discussed in chapter 9). Jesus our priest stands at the boundary between God and humankind, the true mediator, bringing God to us in a saving reconciliation, and us to God in a restored communion with God.

The consequence is not only that we are forgiven from our sins, but also, through our union with Christ, we have a consecrated access into the holy company of God enabling us, in Our Lord's name, to draw near to God in an intimate way, crying, "Abba, Father." In and through Jesus Christ we are able to pray his prayer, making it our prayer: "Our Father, who art in heaven . . ." Christ effects, then, what Calvin called 'a wonderful exchange' (*Inst.* IV.17.2), a glorious substitution, taking to himself our sin, enmity, and death, while giving us his righteousness, love, and eternal life, in sum, his communion with the Father in the power of the Holy Spirit.

"The Church's One Foundation Is Jesus Christ Her Lord"

The three points emphasized are these:

- Jesus is Lord.
- We know this through the witness of the scriptures and the creeds.
- God in Christ loves us unilaterally and unconditionally, forgives us our sins, and restores us to communion with the Father.

The affirmation is cosmic indeed! Every knee (not just Christian knees) should bend, and every tongue (not just Christian tongues) confess, Jesus Christ is Lord, to the glory of God the Father (Phil. 2:10–11). As Lord, Jesus Christ is our life (Matt. 10:39). We are chosen in him from the foundation of the world (Eph. 1:4). We are washed in the blood of the Lamb (Rev. 7:14). God has rescued us from the power of darkness and transferred us into the kingdom of his beloved Son, in whom we have redemption, the forgiveness of sins (Col. 1:13–14). We are born again in and through Jesus Christ into a living hope (John 3:3; 1 Peter 1:3). We have died and risen with Christ so that we are dead to sin and alive to God in Christ Jesus (Rom. 6:1–12). As we wait for a new heaven and a new earth (2 Peter 3:13; Rev. 21:1), we have every blessing in the heavenly places (Eph. 1:3).

The Church faithful with one voice throughout the centuries invites all people to come and see what God has done (Luke 2:15) and to behold the Lamb of God, our living Lord Jesus, who brings us home to the Father (John 14:6).

These facts of salvation are rooted in the Lordship of Jesus Christ. We give thanks to God for this gospel and we rejoice in it. These truths are not negotiable. In the center of this faith, every other point of view or approach to theology must be developed and judged. This content of the gospel is to be proclaimed. God's gracious truth is to be received with gratitude. Thus we encourage all Christians to be bold in their affirmation of Jesus Christ, Lord. With the church in all ages boldly we assert, "There is salvation in no one else, for there is no other name under heaven given among mortals by which we must be saved." (Acts 4:12)

5

The Communion
of the Holy Spirit

Although doctrines are the subject of this book and are very important, the Christian faith does not ultimately consist only of them. To be Christian means to live in the mind (1 Cor. 2:16) and spirit (Rom. 8:9) of Jesus Christ. This chapter focuses on the basic Christian belief in the Holy Spirit, the Third Person of the Holy Trinity, whose principal work is to join us to Jesus Christ, and consequently to one another as the Body of Christ.

Several years ago I was asked to preach on Pentecost Sunday. I began to prepare by pondering the question, "What is the real meaning of Pentecost?" My title was "Jesus Christ: The True Lord of Pentecost," and my theme was that the Holy Spirit is sent to bind us to Jesus Christ. The Holy Spirit is Christ-referring, not self-referring; to say 'Pentecost' and 'Holy Spirit' is to say 'Jesus Christ.' Any spirit that does not lead us to confess 'Jesus is Lord' is not the Holy Spirit of God, but an alien spirit.

One week later I entered the magnificent, roomy pulpit with its blood-red parament in recognition of Pentecost Sunday. Long, red banners hung on the stone sanctuary walls, and red sweaters, red ties, red dresses—indeed, red everything—were scattered among the congregation. Wearing something red had obviously been emphasized. This congregation was set to celebrate the Holy Spirit. And I was about to preach on Jesus Christ.

I preached my sermon aggressively. Moments later, greeting the people at the church door, I was, frankly, feeling a bit smug that I had been so clever in the development of my theme. Thus I was not pre-pared for a young woman who approached me with a strong edge of anger. Her exact words are forgotten, but their intent has remained. I was scolded in no uncertain terms for daring to take away the special day of the Holy Spirit by preaching Jesus Christ. I had, she charged, so "Christianized" the Holy Spirit that she, a woman who was more attracted to a theology that emphasized the Spirit of God in nature than my Christ-centered approach, was deeply offended.

The Christian tradition unambiguously asserts the Personhood of the Spirit in order to deny that the Spirit is merely a force emanating from God, but is rather God with and for us. As God is personal, so the Spirit, as God, is personal. Indeed, the Council of Constantinople in 381 insisted on this reality by asserting not only that the Son but also the Holy Spirit was of one substance or of one being with the Father. As God is holy, so God's Spirit is holy.[1] Yet as God, God's Holy Spirit has to be understood with a Christian specificity. The Holy Spirit must be understood in relation to Jesus Christ and to the work of Jesus Christ. The angry young woman did not understand the cru-cial truth that the Christ-referring nature of the Holy Spirit must be affirmed. Danger lurks in all "Spirit talk" of inferring a generic idea of God's Spirit rather than the Holy Spirit who is of the Godhead, the Father, the Son, and the Holy Spirit, and whose glorious work in the economy of salvation is to bind us to Jesus Christ. In other words, the doctrine of the Holy Spirit is part of the Christian doctrine of God, the Christian doctrine of reconciliation, and the Christian doctrine of the mission of the gospel in and through Jesus Christ.

According to Karl Barth, the Holy Spirit "is the power in which Jesus Christ is alive among these men and makes them His wit-nesses."[2] In other words, Christian doctrine teaches that the work of the Holy Spirit is a Christ-related event, and as such, it becomes a God-glorifying, person-empowering, and church/mission-creating event. Or, to put that in a different way, because the Holy Spirit binds us to Jesus Christ, we are bound by the same Spirit to share in Christ's communion with and mission from the Father.[3] As such, the Spirit calls the Church into existence to be a community of worship and ministry. Thus when we speak of the communion of the Holy Spirit we mean the communion-creating work of the Holy Spirit: commun-ion with the Father through our Spirit-led union with Christ, and consequently communion with one another as we are formed into the missionary Body of Christ, the church. Thus we do not speak of communion *in* the Holy Spirit, but the communion *of* the Holy Spirit, meaning communion *in Christ*.

This chapter explores the communion of the Holy Spirit in three ways, each of which enfolds into the others. First, we will consider the communion between Jesus and the Holy Spirit. Second, we will discuss the work of the Holy Spirit, who brings us into union with Christ, and through him into communion with the Father. The third aspect of the communion of the Holy Spirit we examine is the communion of the Body of Christ, the Church, and the missionary task that is her constitution as she shares through union with Christ in his mission from the Father.

Jesus and the Holy Spirit

Today evidence grows of dissociating the work of the Holy Spirit from Jesus Christ, as was shown with the young woman in the opening story. She believed in a general, generic, or perhaps even non-Christian Holy Spirit. This same view is found also in aspects of the charismatic movement, where so much emphasis is placed on the gifts of the Spirit that the work of Jesus Christ and our union with him may be neglected. In the New Testament the Holy Spirit and Jesus Christ are inseparably connected. In the first place, the Spirit creates the Son. Matthew 1:18 and 1:20 teach that the child conceived in Mary's womb is "from the Holy Spirit." One good reason that the conception by the Holy Spirit and the virginity of Mary are valuable articles of faith (and not theologically irrelevant legends) is that they make the vital connection between Jesus and the Spirit from the very beginning. Jesus was not a man who was later gifted and empowered by the Spirit in a manner similar to others, only more so (although he was anointed by the Holy Spirit at his baptism). He is connected to the Holy Spirit at first hand and from his conception.[4]

Second, the New Testament teaches that the Holy Spirit is in fact the post-Pentecostal Spirit of Jesus Christ (Phil. 1:19 and Rom. 8:9). The Spirit is the Spirit of God's Son whom the Father has sent forth into our hearts (Gal. 4:6). Theologians especially help us here. According to George Hendry, "The manner in which Paul describes the Christian situation indifferently as 'in Christ' and 'in the Spirit' shows that he drew no distinction between the presence of the Spirit and the presence of Christ."[5] Ray S. Anderson makes the same point:

> In his letter to the Roman Christians, Paul freely uses the phrases 'Spirit of God,' 'Spirit of Christ' and 'Holy Spirit' interchangeably (see Rom. 8:9–11; 9:1). Paul's emphasis is on the experience of the Spirit of Christ as Holy Spirit. Hence he does not stress the essential differentiation between the Holy Spirit and Jesus as Son of God in this context. It is the union of Jesus as Son with the Spirit of God that Paul wants us to understand.[6]

The Christian Pentecost is an event that occurred after Jesus' earthly ministry and crucifixion, and after his resurrection, by which the Spirit that so uniquely attached to Jesus is now given to all Christians. John the Baptist who testified to the One who baptizes with the Holy Spirit anticipates this (Luke 3:16). But it is especially in John's Gospel that the coming of the Spirit is consequent upon the departure of Jesus: "Now he said this about the Spirit, which believers in him were to receive; for as yet there was no Spirit, because Jesus was not yet glorified." (7:39 and also at 16:7) The Spirit will be sent from the Father in the name of Jesus to teach the church all things concerning him (John 14:26). While the experience of faith and the self-understanding of the church have the Spirit of Pentecost as their point of origin and means of empowerment, that Spirit is none other than the presence and power of the resurrected Christ.[7] To cite Anderson again: "It is not the Spirit which provides continuity between the mission of God in Jesus and the church, it is Jesus Christ himself, through the coming of the Holy Spirit."[8] Hendry makes the same point: "The function of the Spirit is essentially subservient and instrumental to the work of the incarnate Christ."[9] The Spirit is the Spirit of Jesus Christ. The work of the Spirit is literally Christ directed and Christ centered, whether before or after the incarnation. The New Testament teaches no work of the Spirit except in relation to the person and mission of Jesus Christ.[10] Thus the Spirit of Pentecost is none other than the reality of the Lord of Pentecost, Jesus Christ.[11]

Karl Barth sums up the argument so far:

> Why is it that He is the Holy Spirit (by definition)? . . . The answer is staggering in its simplicity. He is the Holy Spirit in this supreme sense—holy with a holiness for which there are

no analogies—because He is no other than the presence and action of Jesus Christ Himself.[12]

The Holy Spirit is the third Person of the Trinity through whom Jesus Christ is present within history: drawing Christians to and binding them to himself, to share in his communion with the Father, and leading them to participate in his "horizontal" ministry to the least of the brothers and sisters (Matt. 25:31f). The Spirit is the means by which Christians are 'grafted' into Christ (Rom. 11:17), by which Christians "put on Christ." (Gal. 3:27) In the Spirit we participate in the holiness of Jesus Christ. In the Spirit Christians can be witnesses to Jesus (Acts 1:8). The Holy Spirit is none other than the Spirit of Christ, alive and reigning in power to the glory of God the Father.

The Work of the Spirit in Union with Christ

The foundation of the Christian life is Jesus Christ. Thus, the Christian tradition's teaching of the communion of the Holy Spirit means, first of all, union through the Holy Spirit with Jesus Christ himself. Here we pick up a theme found already in chapter 2, and which, as we said there, recurs throughout the book. Union with Christ is not an imitation of Christ, a life of following the example of Jesus by which Christians became better people. Rather, the Christian life as taught by the Apostle Paul is much more radically and convertingly to be understood as a participation in Jesus Christ's righteousness, holiness, and mission through the bond of the Holy Spirit.

John Calvin understood that our deepest self had to become reconfigured and reconstituted or, to use Calvin's words, regenerated or vivified, through our relatedness to Jesus Christ so that our self received a second birth. Our living as Christians is possible only if God reorders us by turning us in a new direction by uniting us to Jesus. Our twisted humanity turned in on itself must be redirected and re-related by God. In other words, our being and becoming Christian is first of all a divine initiative and not something that can be worked out though our heightened religiosity, morality, activity, or spirituality. As in being forgiven, so also in our being and becoming saints (see chapters 7 and 9). God in Christ through the Holy Spirit provides for us. We are conjoined to Christ by the unilateral work of God through the Holy Spirit—in what Calvin called a 'mystical union' (*Inst.* III.11.10). By the bond of the Holy Spirit we become one with him and thereby partake of his benefits.[13] Calvin's term 'mystical union' parallels Paul's 'in Christ,' meaning that God through the Holy Spirit saves us by engrafting us into Christ.

Central to the argument, then, is the understanding of the Christian life as a union with Christ that entails the Spirit-created participation of the saints in his righteousness and holiness. Through the work of the Holy Spirit, Christ brings us into union with himself, so to share in his own life before and from the Father. The Holy Spirit is the bond—Calvin's word, ambiguous as it is—by which Christ unites us effectually to himself and enables us to share in that which is his by nature. Our being bonded to Jesus Christ is a miracle wrought by the Spirit of God. Says Calvin:

> Perfect salvation is found in the person of Christ. Accordingly, that we may become partakers of it he baptizes us in the Holy Spirit and fire (Luke 3:16), bringing us into the light of faith in his gospel and so regenerating us that we become new creatures (cf. 2 Cor. 5:17); and he consecrates us, purged of worldly uncleanliness, as temples holy to God (cf. 1 Cor. 3:16–17; 6:19; 2 Cor. 6:16; Eph. 2:21). (*Inst.* III.1.4)

Calvin uses a striking series of images to describe the work of the Holy Spirit by which we are united with Christ to share in his benefits. As noted, the Spirit is a bond (*Inst.* III.1.1), uniting us to Christ. The Spirit does this work "by his secret watering" that brings forth the "buds of righteousness." (*Inst.* III.1.3) The Spirit is the "inner teacher by whose efforts the promise of salvation penetrates into our minds, a promise that would otherwise only strike the air or beat upon our ears." (*Inst.* III.1.4) The Spirit is "the key that unlocks for us the treasures of the Kingdom of Heaven." (*Inst.* III.1.4) Clearly Calvin placed a great deal of emphasis on the work of the Holy Spirit whereby or in whom we share in Christ's glorious life as Son of the Father, becoming thereby in him the holy people of God.

As the only Son of the Father, with the Father from before all ages, of whom there never was a time when he was not, he, Jesus Christ, with the Father, in the unity of the Holy Spirit, is God. The

consequence of our union with Christ through the Holy Spirit is that
we share in his communion with the Father. By this sharing, what is
his by nature as Son of the Father becomes ours through grace by
adoption. This transference is the astonishing heart of Christian worship and prayer, whereby through our union with Christ we share in
the filial life of love between the Father and the Son, in the unity of
the Holy Spirit. The words of 1 John 1:3 sum up this relationship, "we
declare to you what we have seen and heard so that you also may have
fellowship with us; and truly our fellowship is with the Father and with
his Son Jesus Christ."

To explore the meaning and depth of this extraordinary love of
God, the Church sometimes uses a technical Greek word from the
fourth-century Greek fathers to describe the mystery of the interior
relations within the Holy Trinity. The word is *perichoresis* (*chora* =
'space' or 'room').[14] This Greek term refers to a way of "coinherence"
by which the Persons of the Trinity dwell in one another in a mutual
way, while remaining distinct from one another. Thus the Church
could speak of three divine Persons in the one God. The Holy Trinity could then be understood as the loving movement of communion
among the three Persons in the sublime, ineffable holiness of the unity
of God's true nature. Staggeringly, this love also goes out to reach us
in Christ, and, through our union with Christ by the Holy Spirit, joins
us back to itself, as it were, so that we share in this divine movement
of love.[15] Thus the center of Christian faith and life is understood to
be our sharing in the love within the Holy Trinity, as the Son adores
the Father in the unity of the Holy Spirit—that is, our union with
Christ by the bond of the Holy Spirit.

Through the Spirit, in Union
with Christ, Communion with One Another

United to Jesus Christ by the bond of the Holy Spirit, sharing in
his life of communion before the Father, we are also thereby joined to
one another in communion as the Body of Christ. In union with
Christ we are the Church. We cannot have Christ as our savior, and
therefore God as our Father, without having the church as our community of faith. The communion of the Holy Spirit therefore means
also the communion of the Body of Christ, and as such, a sharing in

his mission from the Father for the sake of the world. Because the Holy Spirit unites us to Jesus, we belong to his fellowship and share in his continuing ministry of grace to the glory of the Father. Therefore, to share in the communion of the Holy Spirit is to share in the life and ministry of the Church.

Strong words are necessary at this juncture because pluralistic individuality can cause so much confusion. Theologically, to think that communion through the Holy Spirit with the ascended Lord Jesus Christ is possible without being necessarily bonded together with one another as the one, holy, catholic, and apostolic church is utter nonsense. People who assume they can be Christian without attending church and participating in the life and mission of the fellowship simply do not understand the meaning of being joined to Jesus Christ. Communion with Christ involves communion with one another and sharing together in Christ's mission to and for the world. Christianity provides a deeply personal relationship with God but is not thereby individualistic and essentially private. Christian faith is lived as a communion in the Body. A more honest approach to church membership vows and an appropriate exercise of accountability over faithful discipleship should be undertaken. Christians should question the voluntaristic understanding of church life because we are not free agents, but men and women joined to Christ and to one another at the deepest levels of our existence. The church is not a free association of voluntary individuals, but the joyful community of those whom Christ claims as his own and who in the Holy Spirit joins to himself, and who live together as disciples under an obedience that is true freedom.

As the Body of Christ, the Holy Spirit joins us to Christ to share not only in his communion with the Father but also in his mission from the Father. The communion of the Body is the Church that shares in the continuing work of Jesus Christ for the sake of the world. Rooted and grounded in love, and growing up in every way into him who is the Head (Eph. 3:17; 4:13), we share not only in Christ's ministry before the Father but also in his ministry from the Father. Since piety and action are intimately related, Christian discipleship is understood both intensively and extensively as communion with God and as service of God in the life of the world. United with Christ through the bond of the Holy Spirit, the church, in other words, is driven by two imperatives: to worship and to serve.

In union with Christ through the communion of the Holy Spirit, the Church was understood to be inherently a church with a gospel mission. This viewpoint came into Reformed theology in part because John Knox taught it with such force. The original frontispiece to the Scots Confession cited Matthew 24:14—"And this good news of the kingdom will be proclaimed throughout the world, as a testimony to all the nations." Then in the Preface to the Scots Confession of 1560, which oddly is missing from the Presbyterian Church (USA)'s *Book of Confessions*, Knox sets forth the missionary thrust of the Scottish Reformation that has shaped the Reformed tradition ever since:

> The Estates of Scotland, with the inhabitants of Scotland who profess the holy Evangel of Jesus Christ, to their fellow countrymen and to all other nations who confess the Lord Jesus, wish grace, mercy and peace from God the Father of our Lord Jesus Christ, with the Spirit of righteous judgment, for salvation. Long have we thirsted, dear brethren, to have made known to the world the doctrine which we profess.[16]

What is remarkable is that the Scots Confession gives primary importance to the missionary calling of the Church. The heart of Knox's vision held that the church existed above all else to preach Christ to all people for their salvation.

At John 17:18 we read of Jesus praying to the One whom he called "Holy Father": "As you have sent me into the world, so I have sent them into the world." Also at 20:21 we read "As the Father has sent me, so I send you." Jesus' command in John's Gospel is a missionary command. For John, the founding of the church is deeply bound up with the meaning of the resurrection of Jesus. On the evening of the first Easter, the risen Jesus came to the house where the disciples had locked themselves in for fear of attack and arrest, and appeared to them. We understand this scene as John's setting for the commissioning of the church. For John, the immediate consequence of Easter is not merely the forming of a religious fellowship that is in communion with the risen Jesus. That church runs the risk of bending in on itself. The risen Jesus appears to give them his peace, but only as a prelude to their great charge: being sent out to continue Christ's ministry in and for the world. "As the Father has sent me, so I send you." According to John, proper knowledge of the risen Lord necessarily involves a commission to go forth into the world in the name of Jesus, the commission to be Christ's disciple. Sent from the Father, the ministry of Christ becomes, through the bond of the Holy Spirit uniting us to Christ, the evangelical and missionary ministry of the church. The church of the Easter gospel is also and necessarily, then, the church with a gospel mission. This passion lay close to the heart of the Scottish Reformation and has been a vibrant part of Presbyterianism ever since.

The meaning of the communion of the Holy Spirit is thus as follows: in union with Christ, the church is given a mission from beyond herself. The world in its own analysis of its needs does not set the agenda for the church. Jesus Christ does. In the power of the Spirit and in union with himself, he sends the church out, and the parallel with his own sending by the Father in incarnation and atonement is quite remarkable. The job of the church is to be the present form of God in Christ in and for the world. To this end she is given the Holy Spirit, and for this end she is the communion of the Holy Spirit.

The Doctrine of the Holy Trinity:
An Epilogue to Chapters 3, 4, and 5

Shocking perhaps to many Christians but true nonetheless is the fact that the doctrine of the Trinity is not strictly biblical but is essential for Christian faith. Since the word "trinity" does not occur in the Bible, obviously the doctrine is not taught there in a literal sense. However, the doctrine of the Trinity is the single most dramatic example of the church's great need for doctrinal thinking on the basis of scripture, for otherwise we would have no coherent Christian doctrine of God.

The doctrine of the Trinity is the result of centuries of reverent reflection on God's self-revelation as the Father, the Son, and the Holy Spirit. The Bible testifies to the holy reality of the Father, the Son, and the Spirit, and the doctrine of the Trinity was created by human thought intended to protect the divine mystery from human misunderstanding—that is, theologians cannot explain the Trinity but they can seek to avoid the errors that would destroy its mystery. The doctrine is, of course, not the reality, which will always be beyond our comprehension. However, the doctrine of the Trinity is not beyond our confession. We confess that we believe in one God in three persons. The Christian confession begins with God, who is revealed to us as the Father, the Son, and the Holy Spirit.

Some theologians, notably Friedrich Schleiermacher in *The Christian Faith*, published in 1822, treat the doctrine of the Trinity at the end of Christian dogmatics. They assume God can be known as God without the doctrine of the Trinity, for it is only a particular, Christian, human, and therefore nonessential proposition. Other theologians, like Karl Barth in *Church Dogmatics*, treat the doctrine of the Trinity at the very beginning because in that fashion God is actually revealed to Israel and the church.

We cannot analyze this immensely complex and highly technical issue except to say again that this book is not focused on our understanding of God but upon the God whom we (in part) understand because God has revealed himself to us in and through Jesus Christ. That is to say, the God whom we encounter in our lives is graciously revealed in scripture to be the Holy Father (chapter 4), the Holy Son (chapter 3), and the Holy Spirit (chapter 5).

6

A Mid-Course Reflection

Every chapter, except for this one, deals with a specific theological doctrine because our purpose in this book is the presentation of basic beliefs of the Christian faith. We want to pause, though, for a few words about the subject of doctrine itself. We stop here after the first five chapters because reflection on the nature of doctrine is a second-order activity, not the real thing itself. Only after we have set faith in the contexts of our encounter with God and our union with Christ, and have presented the doctrine of God as Father, Son, and Holy Spirit, can we rightly take a few pages to reflect on what we are doing. We began with the subject matter to which doctrine bears witness. In that light we now reflect on the nature of doctrine itself. The content of Christian faith, the love of God in Jesus Christ our Lord, prescribes the nature of doctrine; the nature of doctrine does not determine who God is.

Doctrine is an important consideration for Christians since we are commanded to worship God with the mind (Matt. 22:37, Mark 12:30, Luke 10:27). Christian faith has content. What we believe has a great influence on what we do. Activity is ultimately maintained and directed on the basis of conviction.

In what follows, we offer some reflections on the subject of doctrine. First, we discuss three objections to doctrine. Second, we reflect on the practical importance of doctrine. Third, we offer a short note on the relation between basic beliefs and essential tenets. Finally, we offer an even shorter note on theological method.

Objections to Doctrine

Some people today think that doctrine is irrelevant, that absolute truth claims are immoral, and that denominational distinctions are obsolete.

1. *Doctrine is irrelevant.* For example, the doctrine of the Trinity is claimed as a perfect example of the irrelevancy of doctrine. The proponents of this view argue that little worthwhile for real life can be made out of this central doctrine. God as Father, Son, and Holy Spirit, they argue, may have given a general shape to Christian thought, but what is really necessary today is not the understanding of fusty doctrines, but the moral imperative for action. The reign of justice in the world is the goal, they say, not futile discussions of the existence and attributes of God or the nature of the personhood of Christ as God and human, doctrines that finally affect and effect nothing. Doctrine does not heal the sick, feed the hungry, or bring justice to the oppressed. Doctrine does not grow a congregation or heal a broken marriage. In fact, so the claim goes, the emphasis on beliefs is precisely what misdirects attention from the true duty of human life, which is to change the world for the better. The charge is that theologians have only talked about God while the real and true goal is to change the world.

In response, we insist also on the importance of working for the betterment of the human condition, but for Christians, doctrinal clarity guides the accomplishment of this goal by keeping our action faithful to who God is and what God is up to. A professor of philosophy once insisted that the truly open mind is the truly empty mind. We can say that, with regard to central doctrines, the truly open-minded church becomes the truly empty-headed church because it is guided by nothing. Wheels spin frantically in all directions, but the treads never grip the straight road of faithfulness to God's ministry.

Without the heads of doctrine, which raise our minds to God, the heart of church curves back on itself. When the content of the Gospel is dispelled or diluted, the church, in spite of its moral activism, feeds off itself. Basic doctrine answers the core questions: Who is God? How do we know God? Who saves us? What is our response in faithfulness to be to God? What is our hope? Without such reflection the danger always looms that the absence of Christian doctrine will allow the uncritical avowal of some faddish ideology or pragmatism that is merely self-serving. People who resist the effort of doctrinal thinking are, as George Orwell said, "only raising smoke to conceal their own disbelief from themselves."

2. *Absolute truth claims are immoral.* The second objection to doctrine asserts that Christians have no right to exalt one claim to truth over other claims. Skeptics say that to assert the place and role of specifically Christian doctrine as a witness to absolute truth is impossible because we live now in a world characterized by theological pluralism and philosophical relativism. As a result, even some Christians are unwilling to confess the singular Lordship and sole-saving agency of Jesus Christ, and such reticence has led to an attenuated sense of the authority of scripture and to a radical affirmation of all current lifestyles existing in the culture as compatible with Christian faith.

The argument that we live in a postmodern world entails the claim that no absolute claims to truth can be made. One may choose communities of tradition and discourse, but no one of them has the right to be asserted over another. Christian advocacy is a sin against the ethical norms of diversity and inclusivity, which perhaps explains why evangelism is so difficult for many people today.

The advocates of postmodernity insist that the great, so-called master-narratives of the past would be best forgotten. For example, the demise of the once highly regarded systems of Newton, Freud, and Marx are cited as grand attempts to explain our experiences that have crashed on the rocks of pluralism and relativity. Empires rise and fall, so also, apparently, do systems of thought. Modern attempts to produce a coherent explanation of the world must give way to many partial attempts.

In response, we insist on the central affirmation of the Nicene Creed, that Jesus is one in identity and truth with God. Because there is "no other name under heaven . . . by which we must be saved" (Acts 4:12), Christians stand over and against all postmodern avowals of relativity and proclaim that Jesus is Lord and savior. That this stance may put us beyond the pale of propriety as far as some people are concerned only proves the point that "the message about the cross is foolishness to those who are perishing." (1 Cor. 1:18)

3. *Denominational doctrinal distinctions are irrelevant.* The present situation in American society demonstrates the demise of

denominationalism and with it the interest in the doctrinal distinctiveness that denominations represent. Denominational distinctions
are often felt to be less important than broad doctrinal divisions. In
the mainline Protestant churches, for example, there is an alarming,
and widening, division between conservatives and liberals. Analysis of
this situation continues, and doubtless the causes are complicated and
solutions difficult. Nevertheless, a conservative Presbyterian may feel
more kinship to a conservative Episcopalian (or even a conservative
Catholic) than toward a liberal Presbyterian. One result of this situation is the loss of interest in exploring specific theological insights in
favor of focusing on broader and more general Christian agreements.
Additionally, the modern pattern of moving easily from one denomination to another does not foster loyalty to any one doctrinal tradition.

Our response here is to suggest that a generic Christian, liberal or
conservative, does not exist. Christianity is a traditioned faith. Like it
or not, we stand within distinct historical communities that have kept
the faith and handed it on. As Christians we have family names. Doctrinal distinctiveness ensures rootedness in an expression of Christian
faith that has stood the test of time, and also adds savor and taste to
what would otherwise be a bland, faddish contemporaneity. Postde-
nominationalism may become increasingly a sociological fact of
church life, but if we become cut off from the distinct family traditions
and connections, the loss is ours.

The contrast between the continuing, slow decline of the Christian
churches in the West and the incredible growth of the church in Asia
and Africa, some argue, indicates the futility of doctrinal precision.
We are told that before the middle of the next century Anglo-Saxon
peoples will be in the minority in the United States. One example of
third-world growth will suffice. In 1885 when the first missionary
(Horace G. Underwood) arrived, no Presbyterians lived in Korea.
Today Presbyterian Christians in the United States, whose grandpar-
ents sent the Underwoods, number slightly more than 2 million while
the Korean Presbyterian Church in one hundred years has grown
from zero to 10 million. This western decline may be God's intention,
but perhaps the drop off demonstrates our sinfulness. In any case,
decline should not occur through theological default. A conversion to
pragmatic responses to the present circumstance that are devoid of
theological clarity will mean the continuing loss of Christian identity

in our already theologically confused and compromised denominations. Dare we even insist further that what really is important about our being Presbyterians or Methodists or Episcopalians, etc. , is not in fact the system of government as such, but the family heritage in theology and worship that the system of government seeks to express?

The Practical Importance of Doctrine

In America's pragmatic and technological society, hard thinking is sometimes avoided. Richard Hofstadter made this point several decades ago in his classic book, *Anti-Intellectualism in America*, which included a chapter on religion. Nevertheless, human beings cannot avoid thinking, and thinking rightly about God is a Christian duty. Some people assume all debates over doctrine are trifling and academic, but the concern for doctrine is a practical matter. Doctrine is defined as the church's understanding of God, who God is, what God does, what God requires of us, and for what we may rightly hope. This definition shows immediately how practical doctrine is because the subject matter is the practice of God and the consequences for our lives. In this way, doctrine orders the Christian life by setting our hearts on God, to know God rightly and to serve God truly. Doctrine is of immense practical importance because salvation depends on what people believe and know and do about God and God's mission of salvation.

Among other things, doctrinal work has a history that we cannot ignore. That is, we are not the first Christians to think about being obedient to God in word and deed. Intelligent Christians have lived before us and the church has gratefully preserved their legacy. Christians today are surrounded by a great cloud of witnesses who deserve our respect. A person who turns one's back on the church's accumulated confessions as if he or she were the very first Christian wise enough to know what to believe treads on dangerous ground.

Two examples illustrate this point. The first example occurred during a recent service of baptism when the minister putatively baptized the baby in "the name of the Creator, Redeemer, and Sustainer." According to all the doctrinal canons of all the historic Christian churches, this service was *not* a baptism. Christians are baptized into the name of God, Father, Son, and Holy Spirit. No one is baptized into aspects of the work of God. The words of this minister demonstrate ministerial, historical, and theological incompetence. In avoiding the traditional doctrine of the Trinity, and in particular the doctrine of the Fatherhood of God, this minister reduced God to a job description, a serious act of blasphemy. Thankfully, for that child's sake at least, Protestants believe that baptism is not essential for salvation. Sadly, that child, her family, and the congregation were denied the sacramental means of grace by individual arrogance and doctrinal ineptitude on the part of the minister.

A prominent advocate of contemporary worship and culture-sensitive evangelism provides the second example of radical doctrinal modification and confusion. His great passion is to communicate the gospel in the language and images of the culture and to promote the growth of the church. In terms of numbers and influence, his ministry has been a huge success. Among his suggestions is the recommendation that the cross should be taken out of our churches because it is a negative symbol that puts people off Christian faith. We find a similar view expressed even by evangelicals who want to take the prayer of confession out of worship because reminding people of their sin upsets them. Of course Christians must be aware of the pragmatic effects of worship and evangelism, but surely we cannot jettison the church's faithfulness to the great doctrinal and liturgical traditions that have sustained and guided Christians through the centuries. If Christians remove the cross of Jesus in order to make congregations grow, then they are replacing God's action with their own view of what God should have done. A Christian faith without the cross of Christ means a faith without atonement, a faith that leaves us in our sin, no matter how happy and religious we feel as a result.

One of the great hymns of the Church is St. Patrick's breastplate. Patrick, a fifth-century Irish monk, in lacing his tunic every morning rehearsed the doctrines of the faith as he looped the cord through the material. "I bind unto myself today / The strong Name of the Trinity, / By invocation of the same, / The Three in One, and One in Three." Then follows his recitation of the great doctrines of the faith, as he wrapped himself around, as it were, with the whole armor of salvation. Patrick understood that he could not live the Christian life otherwise than being bound by the great teachings of the Christian faith such as Trinity, Incarnation, baptism into union with Christ, atonement, resurrection, and so on. The issue of doctrine is the issue of faithful believing that produces faithful living.

Confusion with respect to doctrine inevitably leads to confusion with respect to the Christian life and the pastoral practice of the Church. The ferocious fights over doctrine that mark so much of the church's history were conducted not for the sake of a rigid orthodoxy, but for the sake of the needful discipline of true faith for the people of God. All doctrinal theology is eventually and inevitably pastoral theology. We are called, then, to doctrinal and theological commitments. Dangerous shoals reside on both sides of the ark of salvation. Conservatives, who ship out under the colors of confessionalism, can easily sail into an unlovely legalism. Liberals, who steam along with a passion for justice and ethics, may quickly veer off into antinomianism. In either case, many people today, by error or by design, are trying to create a church held together without the sinews of doctrine properly understood. The consequences of doctrinal atrophy will be a falling away from the truth of God revealed in the gospel and from the great heritage of communion with Christians who have gone before.

The issue focuses on truth—indeed on Jesus Christ who is the truth (John 14:6). Christians must recognize that we cannot faithfully serve the mission of Jesus Christ if we are unfaithful in what we believe. While we declare ourselves to be a "church reformed and always being reformed, according to the Word of God," we stand also within the catholicity of the church, holding to "what has been believed, everywhere, always and by all." The apprehension of true doctrine in a Christian context is not unchanging; it is always open to reformation. But neither is true doctrine without boundaries. We are grounded in a great theological tradition that guards and guides us in our worship of God and witness to Jesus Christ today. Quite specifically, on this catholic and evangelical theological tradition the various chapters of this book are founded and toward its basic beliefs this reflection is addressed.

Basic Beliefs and Essential Tenets

Among the many interesting theological debates today is the one concerning primary and secondary doctrines. Most theologians accept this distinction in a general way but differ sharply on its application.

For example, the Roman Catholic emphasis on Mary as "the Mother of God" requires a strong defense of the doctrine of the virgin birth. Protestants, on the other hand, affirm the resurrection as primary and the virgin birth as secondary. In whatever way distinctions among doctrines are worked out in detail, the practice of discrimination is important. The relation between basic beliefs and essential tenets is not easy to specify.

In American Presbyterianism, for example, the Adopting Act of 1729 required the subscription of ministers to the Westminster standards "as being in all the essential and necessary articles, good forms of sound words and systems of Christian doctrine." However, the meaning of the crucial phrase "essential and necessary articles" was left ambiguous. In 1890 the "liberal" Presbyterian, Charles A. Briggs, a professor at Union Theological Seminary (New York), called for a new creed that would set forth the essential and necessary articles of the Westminster Confession and omit all unessential and unnecessary articles. In response the "conservative" General Assembly of 1910 specified five essential and necessary doctrines: the inerrant scripture, the virgin birth, the sacrificial atonement, the physical resurrection, and the supernatural miracles. The assembly also declared other doctrines to be equally essential and necessary but did not identify them.

The [Auburn] Affirmation of 1924 resolved the issue by insisting that to declare certain doctrines "essential and necessary" was to amend the constitution. Moreover, the 1924 statement claimed the five "essential" doctrines as presented included theories about facts. The "facts" (the inspiration of the Bible, the incarnation, the atonement, the resurrection, and the continuing life and supernatural power of Jesus Christ) were accepted by all. However, with regard to the "theories," persons of good character and principles might differ. The Affirmation concludes that the Presbyterian Church should once more exemplify "its historic policy of accepting theological differences within its bounds and subordinating them to recognized loyalty to Jesus Christ and united work for the kingdom of God."[1]

This resolution requires two comments. First, the distinction between fact and interpretation of the fact is notoriously difficult to make, and persons of good character and principles may differ on it. Second, apparently in the 1920s both sides on the issue of essential tenets were willing to assume they were united on loyalty to Christ and working for the kingdom. The conclusion seems to be that theological diversity can be managed so long as theological unity can be maintained. However, when the group norm or basic (or essential or fundamental) assumption or set of assumptions that holds a community together is the question at issue, an entirely different situation results.

We have deliberately avoided here the claim to expound essential tenets and have also omitted a detailed analysis of their meaning and use. The chief reason for our focus on basic beliefs rather than essential tenets is that the discussion of the latter tends to be more polemic than irenic. The concept of essential tenets is too often used to divide believers rather than to unite them. Our purpose is neither polemical nor divisive.

In our view basic beliefs or essential tenets should point to a theological richness rather than a theological reduction. Thus the discussion of the topic requires a theological sensitivity more broadly artistic than narrowly scientific. That is, essential tenets or basic beliefs should not be presented as a rigid set of inflexible propositions to which all must subscribe, but rather as a selected gallery of family portraits with individual variations that all may appreciate. In addition, we are not claiming that the doctrines we discuss are "basic" in the philosophical sense that they provide grounds for belief without needing grounding themselves. Our intent is more confessional than logical. We are concerned here with basic beliefs that make us Christian, as seen through the lens of the Reformed tradition in theology. Basic beliefs are intended to express what being and living as a Christian means. These doctrines do not express all that needs to be said on the issue, for we are not writing a systematic doctrinal theology. Other basic beliefs easily could be added. But we believe we can hardly be Christian without these basic beliefs. The reason for these basic beliefs and not others is that we hope they will address matters arising out of our turbulent times.

A Note on Theological Method

This book is our attempt to address the above issues in a constructive way. We do so by framing each subject for discussion within a pastoral concern. Behind the positive development of each individual doctrine—giving, we believe, the answers to our life's problems—is the conviction that the truth is found in the revelation of God in Jesus Christ our Lord. That he is the way, the truth, and the life is not an optional view for Christians. His Lordship is the conviction, given to us by God, that constitutes the church that is his body. Attempting to be faithful to that conviction is the motivation and purpose of every chapter of this book and, we trust, our lives. In short, in this world of diversity, pluralism, and relativism, the one absolute claim for Christians is that Jesus Christ is Lord. The claim is not made in smug arrogance but in profound humility. Christians recognize that God has not called us into the community of the faithful to please us but to use us. Christians cannot clutch God's promises to themselves and hurl curses at the rest of the world. Our obedience requires among other things the obligation to give an account of what we believe.

Put another way, the need for faith to seek understanding (Anselm) produces the human intellectual discipline called theology, which is based on ordered, but interlocking, relations among (1) the scripture (revelation and response), (2) our theological tradition (history and creeds), (3) the experience of faith (encounter and acceptance), and (4) thoughtful reflection (reason). A detailed and technical definition of these relations is of considerable interest to some, but our purpose in this book is to discuss theological doctrines in a pastoral context, not theological method. To praise (and try to understand) your Beloved is one thing. While not entirely unrelated, analyzing how you know you are in love is another matter.

This chapter has been a "time out" for reflections on the nature and merits of doctrine. Having considered previously encountering God, faith, and the doctrine of God, we return to the main task of the book, presenting basic beliefs. We will consider now the great central doctrines of justification and sanctification, separated with a discussion of the visibility of the Word through the celebration of the sacraments, by which we move from the objective nature of salvation to our appropriation of this through our union with Christ. This exposition sets the stage for the discussion of the particular doctrines of sin, predestination, prayer, and scripture. We conclude with reflections on 'pastoral' issues: lamentation, certainty of salvation, hope, and joy.

7

The Finality of Forgiveness

In chapters 3, 4, and 5 our subject was the "Being" of God revealed as the Father, the Son, and the Holy Spirit. The following chapters will deal with two aspects of the "work" of God in salvation: justification and sanctification, or forgiveness and saintliness, interrupted by a chapter on Word and sacraments as the means of grace by which we move from the objectivity of salvation to its reception. The series of topics that focus on the saving work of God is called the way of salvation (often, as a technical term, in the Latin: *ordo salutis*). Of course God's being and work are not separated except for the convenience of our reflections.

Our purpose in the chapters on justification and sanctification is to make clear that forgiveness cannot be separated from saintliness. Those people who are declared forgiven are also those who are declared saints. Therefore John Calvin called the doctrines of justification (forgiveness) and sanctification (saintliness) "twin graces."

Some years ago I was in charge of the baccalaureate service at the college where I was teaching. This event was an important part of the commencement season. The faculty proceeded into the auditorium behind large confessional banners representing the creeds of Reformed theology. The occasion was solemn, with a very generous honorarium paid for an outstanding preacher.

Among other things, I thought this service was a fine opportunity to celebrate notable ancestors of the Reformed tradition. One year we used the famous prayer of Theodore Beza, which he delivered on September 9, 1561, before the notorious Colloquy of Poissy. These times were stern and perilous for the Protestants of France, and Beza's prayer begins with passion:

> Lord God! Almighty and everlasting Father, we acknowledge and confess before Thy holy majesty that we are miserable sinners, conceived and born in guilt and corruption, prone to do evil, unfit for any good; who, by reason of our depravity, transgress without end Thy holy commandments.

After the worship service two of my friends, professors of psychology and gentle but thoroughly secular humanists, approached me with great puzzlement. "Do you really believe in sin?" they asked. I had grown up attending a Christian church, and not believing in sin had never occurred to me. Adam and Eve sinned in the garden, David sinned with Bathsheba and wrote, "Have mercy on me, O God. . . . my sin is ever before me." (Ps. 51) Paul wrote that everyone falls short of the glory of God. Both the witness of scripture and the testimonies of our lives tell us that we are sinners.

I had always defined sin as an offense against God, but I realized that my psychology friends were not convinced about the existence of God or sin. Without God, no sin can be committed against God, and no need is present for forgiveness from God. For Christians sin and guilt are simply realities of our lives, and therefore we understand Martin Luther's desperate search for a gracious God. Most of us, like Luther, believe we are sinners and want to find the God who will forgive us.

A humorist once described two kinds of Christians: grasshopper Christians and possum Christians. Grasshopper Christians, like the Wesleyans, believe in free will and human choice, so they are always stepping forward to lead the godly life and then sliding back or, as they say, "back sliding." Possum Christians, like the Calvinists, believe in foreordination and divine election. God gives them a strong tail and teaches them how to use it. Possum Christians wrap their tails around a branch of the tree of life, and the devil can shake that tree all he wants, but the possum Christians are not falling out. They hold on to the assurance of faith. On the other hand, the grasshopper Christians spend most of their time in the air. If they are not hopping into heaven, then they are hopping out of heaven. Grasshopper Christians have to hope they will die on the inward hop. Otherwise your heart is more strangely warmed than you might desire.

This story raises the question of whether we by our own actions can slip into or out of salvation. If we can, then we are only forgiven "if." Forgiveness is not final, but is contingent or conditional upon what we do, say, or believe. However, if we can really and ultimately frustrate what God wants for our lives, we have little basis for confidence. The "Murphy's Law" of the spiritual life is "if we can sin, we will sin." Moreover, why would God give us the freedom to destroy God's loving purpose for our lives? In that case the gospel is not good news but a death knell, for we will choose to sin. The gospel would condemn us. The issue is whether we base our assurance of salvation upon God's action or upon our own.

If the words above about free will upset the Wesleyan Methodists, the following section should upset the Westminster Calvinists. Too often the Calvinistic view of God's sovereignty makes God's grace capricious and arbitrary. God becomes a mean-spirited judge, and forgiveness is grudgingly bestowed and narrowly restricted. In this view atonement is limited and people who preach the love and generosity of God are condemned.

A clear illustration occurred in 1825 when a young Scottish minister took over the Parish of Rhu in Argyll. His name was John McLeod Campbell. Very quickly he discovered a major pastoral problem: his people had little assurance of their salvation. They had been taught a theological doctrine of election interpreted through limited atonement in which only some people were chosen to be saved. This approach left people searching anxiously within for the signs of their election. They had no confidence in the love and grace of God or in the final forgiveness of their sins. As McLeod Campbell studied his New Testament, he became ever more convinced that this teaching was undercutting the very foundation of the gospel itself. The gospel was for all people, and its content was the generous, free, unconditional grace of God given for us in Jesus Christ. God in Jesus Christ is a God of love and forgiveness, not of hatred and wrath, and God's great desire is for all people to know him as Father through his Son, Jesus Christ. For his efforts, McLeod Campbell was condemned by the Church of Scotland and expelled from the ministry for preaching a gospel contrary to Westminster Calvinism. Two decades later he brought the fruits of his immense labors on the atonement into print in *The Nature of Atonement*, one of the most important studies ever written on the subject, the heart of which is the argument that "if God provides the atonement, then forgiveness must precede the atonement; and the atonement must be the form of the manifestation of the forgiving love of God, not its cause."[1]

Forgiveness can be approached, then, from two perspectives. One is the perspective of human responsibility, using the so-called free-will argument and placing emphasis on our role in accepting or rejecting salvation. The other perspective comes at the problem from the doctrine of God's sovereign love and the nature of the atonement. The question in either case remains: Are we forgiven? The doctrines of conditional or final forgiveness include within their frames of reference issues that take us to the heart of the gospel.

The Graciousness of God

God's grace for Christians is not an abstract idea floating in and out of our minds. Grace is found in Jesus Christ our Lord. Thus the question of the grace of God concerns the reality, power, and consequence of Jesus Christ. Or, to put it differently, since Christ makes atonement for us, how are we to understand the forgiveness of our sins?

Evangelical faith is built on the view that salvation is 100 percent God's work. In salvation, through forgiveness of our sins, God is sovereign. Opposing any kind of view in which a merited human work of one kind or another is required to complete the equation of salvation, evangelical faith asserts the loving and gracious sovereignty of God over all human acts and responses. This assertion holds true in sanctification as well as in justification. In "you shall be my people" (sanctification) as in "I will be your God" (justification), we operate within the unilateral graciousness of God in and through Jesus Christ. All aspects of our salvation and faithfulness have to be understood in terms of the sovereign generosity of God. As such, the generosity or grace of God in and through Jesus Christ constitutes the framework for a proper understanding of the Christian faith and life.

All too often the Christian life has been understood in terms of the old Catholic image of climbing up to God. The image comes from the medieval church, although Protestants also sing "We are climbing Jacob's ladder." The basic problem is that we are the ones who have to do the climbing. It is a short step from the image of ascent to God to the advocacy of a human component in the economy of salvation that has some degree of merit, of what is known as cooperating grace. The great danger is to approach the Christian life with the infection of a residual human-effort theology lingering in our minds, leading us to suppose that we still have to earn God's favor through our faith or our piety or our good works. The Christian life becomes a way to obtain God's favor. To put the point more succinctly, life becomes a quest to manipulate ourselves into God's good graces.

The alternative view of the Christian life begins with God's overwhelming generosity or liberality that leads to or solicits God's children's answering gratitude. Forgiveness should be understood within the context of grace and gratitude. Human thankfulness is the correlate of God's goodness. A theology of the Christian life will then be a theology of gratitude for God's generosity rather than a theology of duty or obedience to a divine despot.

An extended biblical reflection to support this point would be appropriate here. Romans 5:12–21 is a key passage on the understanding of grace in the New Testament. Romans 5:15 reads: "But the free gift is not like the trespass. For if the many died through the one man's trespass, much more surely have the grace of God and the free gift in the grace of the one man, Jesus Christ, abounded for the many." This statement of the gospel indicates the situation that exists by God's decision and act before any decision and act of ours. The statement speaks to the abundance of divine generosity, enabling us to speak indeed of 'good news.' Generosity, here supremely, becomes the key signature of the gospel.

In Romans 5 Paul draws out the consequence of his perspective on faith that he has just expounded at length. He moves from the particular to the universal. In the first half of the chapter, Paul spells out the consequences of justification for the individual in the present and the future—suffering now with the sure hope of salvation. In the chapter's second half, the language shifts to a different tone altogether in which the whole sweep of human history is embraced in the two epochs initiated by the two figures—Adam and Jesus Christ, respectively—who represent the turning points of history. Here the perspective pulls back from the individual and his or her concerns for salvation to reveal now a cosmic focus that includes all persons in all ages of time. Paul raises his sights to survey the full panorama of history in the light of these two epoch-making figures. Paul presents the scope and expanse of the gospel at the full height of his theological power. But his eloquence is stretched to the breaking point as he struggles to express the generous reality of the grace of God that is inaugurated in the person and work of the second Adam, Jesus Christ.

The contrast between Adam and Jesus Christ, begun in verse 12, taken up again at verse 14, is raised once more at verse 15 to show the difference between the two ages, the age of death and the age of life. For Paul, Christ is the midpoint of history. In Christ we do not just see the irruption of something new into history. Rather, we see the Christ event as the event that totally redefines history on its own terms. A profound distinction manifests itself in a life unto death, on the one hand, and a life unto life, on the other. The gift of grace, Jesus Christ, a free gift, is a concrete embodiment of grace that is contrasted with Adam's disobedience. For by the sins of one man (Adam) many died (referring back to v. 12), so by the gift of grace (Jesus Christ) many are brought to justification (v. 16).[2] The free gift of grace is not like the trespass; the work of Jesus Christ is not proportional to the work of Adam. "If, because of the one man's trespass, death exercised dominion through that one, much more surely will those who receive the abundance of grace and the free gift of righteousness exercise dominion in life through the one man, Jesus Christ." (v. 17) Notice how Paul piles up images to try to express the overwhelming aspect of the power and reality of God's grace: "much more surely," "the abundance of grace," "the free gift." The apparent redundancy of language suggests that Paul is stretching for the abundant free-flowing quality of God's grace in Jesus Christ, the one person who stands in contradistinction to Adam.

Verse 15 ends with the word that catches the attention and points to a sure and certain conclusion concerning God's generosity: the grace "abounded" for the many. In Greek the word is *perisseuo*, which means to overflow or exist in abundance. This word is used quite often by Paul, as for example, at Romans 3:7—God's truthfulness abounds to God's glory; at Romans 15:13—Christians abound in hope by the power of the Holy Spirit; and at 2 Corinthians 9:8—God gives every blessing in abundance leading to an abundance of good works. The word evidently refers to God's generosity in giving. At Romans 5:15, the grace of God overbalances sin. What a remarkable notion that is! Any sense of symmetry or reciprocity between the work of Adam and the work of Jesus Christ is overwhelmed by the extraordinary abundance of grace. Grace overflows. Grace abounds. Grace is extravagant, and it is an amazing grace. God's grace has the quality of "much more surely" or "all the more." Grace obliterates sin and death, overwhelming them with reconciliation between God and humankind. In Christ Jesus life triumphs over death. The grace of God spills over and everything is washed clean. God has given us this gift in Jesus Christ as the new epoch is inaugurated singularly by his person and act. History has been turned on the axis of God's benevolence toward those who had until now been God's enemies. (Romans 5:6)

Surely to insist on the point, Paul uses the same word twice more in the argument. At Romans 5:17 he writes of "those who receive the abundance of grace and the free gift of righteousness." But at Romans 5:20 the word is used most remarkably: "where sin increased, grace abounded all the more." Sin may increase, but again the contrast with grace is asymmetrical, although here now even more wildly and extravagantly. For in a deliberate literary device perhaps lost in English translation, Paul stretches the abundance of grace to a breaking point, using now the superlative form (*hupereperisseuen he charis*). Grace abounds exceedingly—a superabundance of grace, a Niagara Falls of grace. Eugene Peterson paraphrases the meaning beautifully: "But sin didn't, and doesn't, have a chance in competition with the aggressive force we call *grace*. When it's sin versus grace, grace wins hands down."[3]

The point Paul is trying to make is that grace overwhelms everything that is not gracious. Grace sweeps everything before it. For that reason, Reformed Christians refer to the sovereign grace of God with no attempt at theological balance. For in generosity God has unconditionally and unilaterally established communion between God and humankind. More than a gift to be received, grace is an actuality declared. This point of evangelical faith may be hard to grasp. Our ego-need sense of human possibility and empowerment urges us to want to tame the radical nature of grace. Surely we have to do something to play our part? We long to be important, even in matters concerning faith. God most certainly commands our faith and obedience, but always in the context of the generosity of a grace that goes before us, summed up in these words from 2 Corinthians 1:18–20: "As surely as God is faithful, our word to you has not been 'Yes and No.' For the Son of God, Jesus Christ, whom we proclaimed among you, Silvanus and Timothy and I, was not 'Yes and No'; but in him it is always 'Yes.' For in him every one of God's promises is a 'Yes.'"

In view of this superabundance of grace, our understanding of faith and life must be totally recast in such terms, meaning nothing less than the baptism of our reason as well as our actions by grace. Christian faith and life are irrevocably under grace. In terms of this grace, our thinking and living have to be entirely reconfigured whereby we are in fact transformed by grace for the renewing of our lives at the deepest level imaginable (Rom. 12:2 and Eph. 4:23, for example). God's extravagant generosity becomes then the controlling theme of all Christian theology, all Christian ethics, and all Christian life.

The Finality of Forgiveness

The Christian life is lived by those who know they have been forgiven and made perfect by the person and act of God in Jesus Christ. This extraordinary claim means that the Christian life is possible at all only on the basis of the unconditional or sovereign generosity of God. This assertion is found in Hebrews 10:12 and 10:14, for example. Verse 12 reads "But when Christ had offered for all time a single sacrifice for sins, 'he sat down at the right hand of God.'" This verse represents the heart of the gospel of God's salvation, a summary of the work of Jesus Christ in his priestly and royal offices. Verse 14 makes the connection with the Christian life: "For by a single offering he has perfected for all time those who are sanctified."

First, Jesus Christ has made the single sacrifice for sin. The emphasis on his sacrifice as the single sacrifice for sin obliterates any role in atonement now to be borne by us. The utter graciousness is astonishing, the continuing reality of Good Friday in our lives. Jesus Christ has taken on himself the sins of the whole world and restored us to a new and acceptable relationship with God. The New Testament tells us that this sacrifice amounts to a new creation (Gal. 6:15; 2 Cor. 5:17; John 3:3f).

Jesus Christ is the sole mediator between heaven and earth,

between God and humankind. He has borne the cost and judgment for sin. As Paul put it, "while we were still weak, at the right time Christ died for the ungodly." (Rom. 5:6) When God looks at us, we who remain in ourselves always the ungodly, God sees us in the light of Jesus Christ and his sin-offering of himself for us. God looks at us from the perspective or through the lens of the cross. Therefore no other sacrifice for sins needs now to be made. The sacrifice has been offered vicariously and finally: a past completed act whose influence spreads forwards and backwards to embrace all history and all people in its staggering mercy and inclusivity. We have to take the 'all things' (*ta panta*) of Ephesians 1:10 seriously. As Jesus said on the cross, "It is finished." (John 19:30) The work of overcoming the horrendous gulf between God and us caused by our sin has been completed. Sin is forgiven for all time, so Paul can joyously celebrate this great fact of faith: "I am convinced that neither death, nor life, nor angels, nor rulers, nor things present, nor things to come, nor powers, nor height, nor depth, nor anything else in all creation, will be able to separate us from the love of God in Christ Jesus our Lord." (Rom. 8:38–39) Christ's sacrifice is adequate and final. We are forgiven. The whole drama of atonement is the great sign of the saving generosity of God.

This point may be illustrated with a bad theological joke. God and the Devil are having a conversation and the Devil pokes God in the ribs saying, "Do you see that Christian over there committing a sin?" God looks but replies that he sees no sin. The Devil thinks that a bit odd, but carries on the conversation. A little later, the Devil again pokes God in the ribs. "Do you see it now? There is that Christian again committing a terrible sin." Again God looks and replies that he sees no sin. A third time God is poked in the ribs by the Devil. "This time you must have seen the awful sin committed by that supposed Christian of yours. In your justice and holiness you have to punish him." God looks, and replies again that he sees no sin. In unrighteous indignation and exasperation the Devil insists that sin was committed. "Why can't you see the sin?" the Devil asks God. To which God replies, "Because Jesus is standing in the way!" Jesus is our Savior because he is always standing between us and the wrath of God.

The text from Hebrews states that Jesus then sat down at the right hand of God. To read this statement as mythological and irrelevant to the proper understanding of atonement and God's faithfulness is tempting. But to do so would mean missing its theological and pastoral significance. On the one hand, the image implies that the sacrificial work of Jesus, his work as priest, is now over. On the other hand, this image implies that the Jesus who made the one sacrifice for sins is now the royal ruler. He has a continuing role to play and therefore a future. The one who was priest and victim, the Good Friday Lord, is now the Royal One who rules the universe, the Easter and Ascension Lord, who must yet turn all that is in his care over to his Father (1 Cor. 15:24–28), where again we encounter "all things" (*ta panta*). The universe and its future are in the care of the one who died for our sins. The derelict, forsaken man hanging in disgrace upon a cross on a hill outside Jerusalem is here seen to be both sin-bearer and king-ruler. Good Friday, Easter Sunday, and Ascension Day all come together in this verse. Who we see Jesus to be for us on the cross is also who God in Jesus Christ always chooses to be through Jesus' eternal rulership over the universe. Jesus' royal rule at the right hand of the Father means that God always is for us.

This theological insight was also expressed by Paul. "Who is to condemn? It is Christ Jesus, who died, yes, who was raised, who is at the right hand of God, who indeed intercedes for us." (Rom. 8:34) The Nicene Creed also echoes this assertion with the familiar words: "He (who descended into Hell) ascended into heaven and is seated at the right hand of the Father. He will come again in glory to judge the living and the dead, and his kingdom will have no end." Thank God that Jesus Christ is our judge!

The course of our salvation is not in our efforts to climb up to God. Our piety does not give us the key to the kingdom of heaven. Even our decision for Jesus, an image so beloved by evangelicals today, is of no ultimate account in the economy of salvation. What saves us is God's decision and act in and through Jesus Christ to do for us what we cannot do for ourselves, namely, to bear the cost of sin-separation from God and to restore us to communion with God. The consequence of election is that "he chose us in Christ before the foundation of the world to be holy and blameless before him in love." (Eph. 1:4) Not what we feel, not what we decide, not what we think, not what we do, not what we believe: nothing from our side saves us. All that saves us is what God does in Jesus Christ: election, justification, and sanctification. He alone has done what is complete, adequate, and eternal. In

Jesus Christ we are the forgiven sons and daughters of God, and as such, people who have been brought home to God.

Although we will discuss holiness (sanctification) in a later chapter, saying just a few words would be appropriate now. The text from Hebrews 10 continues at verse 14: "For by a single offering he has perfected for all time those who are sanctified." Here the transition is made from justification to sanctification. The great work of reconciliation does not stop with forgiveness. The sovereignty of God embraces our response as much as it determines God's act. To be forgiven is one thing; to be turned back to God in conversion and discipleship as the church of Jesus Christ is yet something else. People who are forgiven must yet become the saints of God, the faithful ones.

The danger of misunderstanding is great at this point. Far too often is the presumption made that this second stage in the economy of salvation is entirely human. That is, we take over the project of reconciliation and through our own will and acts complete the equation of our redemption. We discuss this topic further as condign merit in the chapter on prayer. The point is to beware the temptation to rely on human effort and limit the range of God's grace. Scripture does not suggest we can sanctify ourselves. According to Karl Barth, the New Testament "knows nothing of a Jesus who lived and died for the forgiveness of our sins, to free us as it were retrospectively, but who now waits as though with tied arms for us to act in accordance with the freedom achieved for us."[4] As we shall see in chapter 9, our sanctification is also a matter of God's special grace. That is, the sovereign generosity of God does not end with atonement, but carries into our living the Christian life. That Jesus Christ is our sanctification as well as our righteousness and redemption (1 Cor. 1:30) can hardly be overemphasized. God demands our living the amended life as Christians because we are already saints of God in Jesus Christ to whom we are united.

Whatever else we say, God's grace is not cheap, mean, or cautious. Neither are Christians to be cheap, mean, or cautious in our expressions of gratitude for grace. For the Christian, all life is controlled by the generosity of God so that even the structures of our minds and the patterns of our wills are converted and bent back into shape by the action of God's grace upon them. According to the apostle Paul, "We have the mind of Christ" (1 Cor. 2:16), and similarly at Philippians 2:5, "Let the same mind be in you that was in Christ Jesus." In statements like these Paul is trying to capture the magnitude of the conversion wrought by grace. God's extravagant generosity to us in Jesus Christ extends to our final forgiveness and thus becomes the controlling theme of all Christian theologies, all Christian ethics, and all Christian life.

8

The Visibility of the Word

One of my most vivid experiences of a specific encounter with the living Lord Jesus occurred one Easter Season at a Communion service in the Abbey on Iona, Scotland. Shivering in the barely heated, restored eleventh-century church, around a Communion table hewn from ancient green Iona marble, I was alone with a mere handful of other pilgrims. Suddenly I became aware of both the presence of the living Lord Jesus Christ and the hosts of men and women who had worshiped through the centuries in this ancient place. The sense of ancientness, perhaps, led to my intuitive awareness. Explanations aside, this awareness was that Jesus was Lord, that he was alive, and that I was gathered with the church in heaven and on earth in a personal communion with him. The Lordship of Jesus Christ is not a theoretical construct but a truth, attested in scripture and known in a personal encounter with our living Lord, who is made visible to us in the sacraments of baptism and the Lord's Supper.

Because the sacraments are public actions, many questions surround their practice. For example, an adult, baptized as an infant, at the instruction of his pastor insists now on a believer's baptism through immersion; another person, baptized and believing, is denied Holy Communion because she is outside the communion of that denomination. When is a baptism valid or invalid? What is the correct way to be baptized? What is required for one to be accepted at the Lord's Table? Who is authorized to celebrate these sacraments, and what happens when the celebration is done?

In the popular mind John Calvin is an excessively logical thinker who did not flinch from making harsh deductions based on his view of the Bible. This caricature of Calvin as a "theo-logician" is nowhere better exposed as false than in his profound conviction that the Lord's Supper is more to be adored than understood (*Inst.* IV.17.32). In the course of this book, frequent appeal is made to mystery and adoration, which is especially appropriate in this chapter dealing with what Christians understand about the sacraments. Clearly adoration cannot be separated from understanding, however, because head and heart go together.

God's grace comes to us in many ways. Calvin remarks that God's providence (1) sometimes works through an intermediary, (2) sometimes without an intermediary, and (3) sometimes contrary to every intermediary (*Inst.* I.17.1). In other words, God sometimes uses certain instruments or means to accomplish the divine purpose. Sometimes God acts directly and immediately. Sometimes God brings about results that are not naturally produced by those instruments. Our union with Christ in this regard is God's direct action. Not willing to restrict God's freedom, Reformed theology confesses that God's grace can be mediated to us by *extraordinary* means. Karl Barth insisted, for example, that "God may speak to us through Russian Communism, a flute concerto, a blossoming shrub, or a dead dog."[1] However, God is orderly and the *ordinary* means of grace are two—the preaching (and hearing) of the Word and the celebration (and reception) of the sacraments. The divine action of God, including the revelation of our union with Christ, is normally revealed to us by Word and sacraments. While God's freedom is unbounded, human beings are bound by the ordinary means of grace.

In Reformed theology the two means of grace are also the identifying marks of the true church, although Christian discipline is sometimes added as a third (see The Scots Confession, chapter XVIII). Protestants dismissed the Roman Catholic claims for seven sacraments because in the New Testament our Lord Jesus Christ only instituted two sacraments, baptism and Eucharist. Word and sacrament belong together, which means that Christians are not allowed to choose one and ignore the other. Sometimes a tradition will emphasize one at the expense of the other. The Latin Roman tradition, for example, tends to emphasize the Holy Communion at the expense of preaching the Word of God, forgetting that the Word orders and governs the sacraments. Protestants, on the other hand, have sometimes emphasized a preaching church, with only infrequent eucharistic celebration. This approach is in contrast to the Scottish Reformer John Knox, who, in 1560, advocated weekly celebration of Holy Communion. He also took the Communion table from the top end of the High Kirk of St. Giles in Edinburgh and placed it below the pulpit, which is situated along the side of the left wall in the middle of the building. Knox repositioned the table to signal Word and sacrament in the closest possible conjunction. The sacraments enact the sermon, as it were, for they are the Word of God given for the people under the elements of water, bread, and wine. The Word of God is not mere ideas, but the living word in both aural and corporeal form. The sermon expounds the meaning of the sacraments, so that they are not seen as magic. Word and sacraments are central to the life and mission of the church. As such, they are "the ordinary means of grace" in Christian tradition.

Preaching presents the *invisible* Word of God to the ear and mind and heart of the company of the faithful. The sacraments, the *visible* Word of God, appeal to the eye and heart and mind. Both forms of the means of grace are essential to Christian faith and life. Word and sacraments are God's ordinary way of nurturing us into relationship with him. In the preaching of the Word we hear the address of God interpreted for our lives. According to the Second Helvetic Confession the preaching of the Word of God *is* the Word of God (chapter I). Baptism is the recognition of our engrafting into Christ, and the reception of his righteousness because of our union in Christ, which is the motivation for our faithful obedience. The Lord's Supper provides continual spiritual nourishment that we may grow strong in faith.

The Word and sacraments are intended to secure and nurture Christians in their union with Christ. By these primary modes of God's presence, God through the Holy Spirit joins us to Jesus Christ. Nevertheless, in the churches the Word and sacraments are still sources of confusion and conflict. During the Reformation, Protestants generally agreed about the importance of preaching and the interpretation of baptism. (The Anabaptists, to be discussed later in this chapter, were exceptions regarding baptism.) However, the doctrine of the Lord's Supper was fiercely debated, and the disagreements remain even today.

This chapter will discuss first the general agreement on the doctrine of baptism, then briefly explore four views of the Eucharist, and finally examine the doctrine of the Lord's Supper in Reformed theology.

Baptism

Many ways exist to misunderstand the sacrament of baptism. For example, a grandmother approached me quietly after Sunday service and asked me to baptize her grandson the following Sunday before he and his parents made a cross-country trip by airplane. On another occasion I received a phone call to rush to the maternity wing of a hospital where a parishioner's newborn baby had taken a turn for the worse. In each case the mother and grandmother thought that without baptism the babies were not properly protected from physical danger. This view is of baptism as talisman, as magic.

Baptism is a sacrament established by God to celebrate our initiation into the name of God. Children and adults are baptized into the name of the Father and the Son and the Holy Spirit. Baptism is a once-for-all event that bears witness to our union with Christ. *The Scots Confession* states, "We assuredly believe that by Baptism we are *engrafted into Christ Jesus*, to be made partakers of his righteousness, by which our sins are covered and remitted." (chapter XXI, emphasis added) Baptism is grounded in the act and promises of God and not in the needs and desires of individuals. Baptism is God's action.

Baptism is a work of the Triune God through the instrumentality of the church: the Holy Spirit engrafts us into Jesus Christ to have communion with the Father through him. By baptism we are enfolded into the life of God, to share through our union with Christ in the communion of love that is the nature of God. As the New Testament makes clear again and again, only through our incorporation into Christ by the Holy Spirit do we come to the Father. Baptism is not merely an outward symbol that God loves us or that we are members of the church. Baptism is a public exhibition of a reality that we have been named and claimed by God in and through our union with Christ to be God's covenant partners by sharing in Christ's own life before the Father.

Baptism is God's sign to us that our sins are forgiven. To be engrafted into Jesus Christ through baptism is, as Paul says, to become a sharer in his death (Gal. 3:3). Through baptism we become sharers in the power of his atonement, which means the covering and remission of our sins. To be baptized means that by faith through grace we trust in the forgiveness of our sins. The waters of baptism signify the washing away of our sins. We must hold in tension here a twofold mystery that cannot be readily resolved. First, baptism means we are forgiven before we have sinned, but still we are called to repent and make amendment of life, though the repentance and amendment of life are also gifts of the Holy Spirit. Second, many baptized persons who sin do not repent. Thus grace and mercy contained in baptism can be rejected. Baptism, in Calvin's arresting image, can lie neglected (*Inst.* IV.15.17). Salvation is not automatic for those who are baptized. The indicative of baptism calls forth obedience to the imperatives of faith and faithfulness, and failure on that account is dire indeed. The paradox is between the work of God on the one hand and human responsibility on the other. This mystery is to be received with gratitude and obedience rather than logically explained.

Infant baptism is again a source of controversy in the church today. Some Christian groups, continuing the views of the Anabaptists of the Reformation period, insist on believer's baptism only. That is, only those persons who can affirm their faith can be baptized. Obviously, infants are disqualified.

This view is correct insofar as believers' baptisms are proper *if believers are not already baptized.* In a missionary environment such as North America is fast becoming, when fewer children are baptized as babies, believer's baptism will probably become more and more common. Further, as theologians such as Karl Barth and Jürgen Moltmann have insisted, the baptism of children is now so often an expression of cultural Protestantism, a routinized rite of passage, that the act is really an offense to the true sacrament. The argument is rightly made that the church must exercise appropriate discipline over baptism to ensure that infants baptized into Christ indeed are brought up within the Body of Christ. Baptism calls for the Church to be held accountable for the faithful keeping of the promises made at baptism.

However, the argument for believers' baptism is incorrect when it means *re*baptism. Our incorporation into Christ can happen only once. As the secret work of the Holy Spirit, baptism cannot be lost. A person baptized as an infant comes to confessing faith by a mystery of God's providence. Not all who are baptized become believers. For whatever reason, they willfully and stubbornly reject the internal grace of the Holy Spirit. Yet people who do come to faith enter into the promises already contained in their baptism. That one lays active claim later in life to one's baptism is a ground not for rebaptism but for celebration and thanksgiving that God has brought the promises of baptism to pass in a particular life. The emphasis is properly placed on the act and promises of God rather than on the subjective experiences of the believer. In this way we understand that baptism is given for faith, not faith for baptism.

Four Views of the Lord's Supper

On their doctrines of the Lord's Supper, Christians are still divided along lines formed in the sixteenth century. This "supper-strife" would be even more evident today if Protestants knew their theology better. One reason for neglecting this contentious subject is the worthy desire to be ecumenical that has caused many Christians to avoid putting much emphasis on confessional distinctiveness. However, tolerance of theological diversity will always fail when irreconcilable conflict is present at the deepest and most persistent levels of individual and community faith and life. Since Christians were divided on the doctrine of the Eucharist the various views were attacked by some and defended by others. As no reconciliation appeared possible between the Protestant and the Roman Catholic doctrines of the Lord's Supper, several irreconcilable Protestant views emerged as well.

Not only much ink but also much blood has been spilled over strongly held interpretations of the Lord's Supper. The subject is complicated, the history complex, and the results immense. A brief explanation suggests that (1) the Catholics taught transubstantiation, (2) the Lutherans taught consubstantiation, (3) the Zwinglians taught no presence, and (4) the Calvinists taught real presence.

In understanding the Eucharist, Roman Catholic theology depends on the philosophy of the Greek philosopher Aristotle, and specifically his view of substance and attributes. While the attributes of bread and wine stay the same, a miracle occurs to change the substance of the bread and wine into the body and blood of Christ. This change of substance is called transubstantiation. The Lutheran view, called consubstantiation, answers the same question, "How is Christ present in the Lord's Supper?" but in a slightly different way. Christ is present, according to Lutherans, in, with, and under the physical elements of bread and wine. This position depends on the conviction that the ascended Christ is ubiquitous, meaning he is everywhere present. Thus he is bodily present in, with, and under the bread and wine. The Zwinglian view maintained that both the Catholic and Lutheran doctrines were pure superstitions. The true answer to the question of Christ's physical presence in the Eucharist is that he is not present. The risen Christ sits at the right hand of God the Father Almighty. The Lord's Supper is, then, a memorial meal only. This view is very common in "low church" North American Protestantism.

John Calvin believed, against the Zwinglians, that Christ is really present in the Lord's Supper, but he insisted, against the Catholics and Lutherans, that Christ is not enclosed within the elements of bread and wine. According to Calvin, Christ was raised from the grave in his physical body and ascended into heaven with our humanity. Thus, and for our benefit, Christ is "locally present" at the right hand of God in his continuing humanity. However, since Jesus Christ is and remains both fully human and fully divine, he is present in the Lord's Supper by the power of the Holy Spirit. According to Reformed theology the real presence of Christ in the Eucharist is the work of the Holy Spirit.

The Eucharist in Reformed Theology

Reformed theology takes its eucharistic theology seriously and understands that the Lord's Supper is for sinners. I learned this lesson as a seminarian on a summer internship in the western highlands of Scotland, ministering in the town of Kilchoan on the beautiful Ardnamurchan peninsula. Westminster Calvinism is especially strong in this area. Among my pastoral duties was a regular visitation with a retired captain who had served in the merchant navy, and who now lived quietly in this Gaelic-speaking parish. He rarely missed church on Sunday morning, but never received Holy Communion at the quarterly celebration. One Communion Sunday I was astonished to see him participate in the Eucharist. A pastoral visit later in the week led to the discovery that the old man had hitherto felt he was not worthy to participate in the holy meal. Now, near the end of his days, he confided in me, somewhat shyly, that he did feel worthy to receive the bread and the cup. Reluctant to contradict such a serious and austere gentleman, I thought but did not say how terribly sad it was that all his faithful life he had felt unable to commune with his living Lord because he had been taught, wrongly, that Holy Communion is for the righteous and not for sinners. The fact is, none of us is ever worthy to come to the Lord's Table except as we are united to him and participate in his righteousness, trusting never in our own merit.

The Lord's Supper is a real communion with the living Lord. In the Lord's Supper we participate in a communion with the Father, through the Son, in the power of the Holy Spirit. Calvin says that "our souls are fed by the flesh and blood of Christ in the same way that bread and wine keep and sustain physical life. . . . Christ pours his life into us, as if it penetrated into our bones and marrow." (*Inst.* IV.17.10) In the bread and wine of the sacrament we really do feed upon the living Jesus Christ. The elements are not just bare signs, nor the Communion a ritual that reminds us of spiritual truths. The elements exhibit the means of grace by and through which Christ is really spiritually present for us in our physical world. Calvin calls Holy Communion "a true participation" in Christ that leads to our growing into one Body with him, that we may know his power directly and thereby enjoy his benefits (*Inst.* IV.17.11).

Nothing magical happens to the bread and the wine. They do not outwardly appear to be one thing, while actually becoming something else. Protestants reject the metaphysics of the Roman Mass, which claims that the elements become actually and physically the body and blood of Christ while appearing to be bread and wine, and the concomitant theology of the priesthood. The bread and the wine are and remain the physical realities by which Christ offers us his body and blood. The mystery of grace in the sacrament takes place spiritually in the power of the Holy Spirit, not by some change in the elements. The miracle of Holy Communion is spiritual.

For Protestants the singular point of importance is the actual spiritual communion that we receive with Jesus Christ when we eat the bread and drink the wine of the Holy Communion: a thorough spiritual joining of Christ and ourselves by an act of the Holy Spirit. By the Spirit, and through the elements, we share in the life of the living Lord Jesus, to receive him into ourselves. The emphasis is properly placed on the transformation of the believer through this sacrament, the outworking of the union with Christ to which baptism bears witness. In and through its sharing in the Lord's Supper, the church is maintained in her union with Christ. Calvin notes that almost the entire force of the sacrament lies in these words: "which is given for you," and "which is shed for you." (*Inst.* IV.17.3) The consequence is a confirming of the promise of life in, with, and through Jesus Christ. In this way, through flesh and blood, Christ continues to order the church in its life of deepening faithfulness to the gospel. On this ground the case is most assuredly to be made for the frequent celebration of the sacrament.

The Lord's Supper is the sign of what Calvin called "the wonderful exchange," which we mentioned in chapters two and four. One of the most glorious paragraphs in the whole of Calvin's *Institutes of the Christian Religion* is the paragraph entitled *Union with Christ as the special fruit of the Lord's Supper.* (IV.17.2) Calvin teaches that we share in our Lord's life before and with the Father as he takes what is ours and gives us what is his. This sharing leads to the assurance that eternal life, of which he is the heir, is ours; that the kingdom of heaven into which he has entered cannot be cut off from us; and that, since we are absolved from our sins because he took them upon himself, we cannot now be condemned. This, says Calvin, "is the wonderful exchange which, out of his measureless benevolence, he has made with us; that, becoming Son of man with us, he has made us sons of God with him." Thus, by his descent to earth, Jesus Christ has prepared our ascent to heaven. By taking on our death, he has conferred his life upon us. By accepting our weakness, he has strengthened us by his power. By receiving our poverty, he has given us his wealth. By taking the oppressive weight of our sin upon himself, he has clothed us with his own righteousness.

Conclusion

The meaning of sacraments is quite revolutionary for our lives. By the Holy Spirit, through our union with Christ, given in our baptism and renewed continually through the Lord's Supper, that which is ours—our broken, confused, ambiguous lives—are taken by our Lord and made whole, as he offers our lives to the Father in his own name and for his own sake. And he takes his own life of perfect unity with the Father and communicates it to us, so that in, with, and through him we share in his life in and before God. What is ours becomes his; what is his becomes ours. This wonderful exchange is at the center of Christian faith and life and is the special fruit of the Lord's Supper.

The sacraments are God-given outward public ordinances of the church that bear witness to the spiritual reality of our union with Christ, both our being joined to him and our growing into him. Baptism is the basis for Holy Communion, and Holy Communion is the fulfillment of the promise of baptism. Word and sacrament belong together. The sacraments enact the sermon because they are the Word of God made visible and given for the people through the elements of water, bread, and wine. The Word of God is not merely conveyed to us invisibly, but in God's grace the Word becomes visible in the sacraments. This Word of God in sermon and sacrament is not something other than God. The Word of God is God's living presence in speech and act, which is none other than Jesus Christ himself, our savior. To speak God's Word is to say Jesus Christ, God's Word incarnate, crucified, risen, and ascended. To celebrate the sacraments is to enact God's saving relationship with us in and through Jesus Christ whereby we are engrafted into God and grow more fully into that communion. God's Word is Jesus Christ, who is the subject of sermon and sacrament.

9

The Struggle for Saintliness

On my door at Pittsburgh Theological Seminary is a cartoon, drawn by a pastor, that shows a fierce questioner asking, "Are you Holy?" To which I reply, "Who me? No. I'm Church of Scotland." This small story summarizes the answer of many people who are more than a little nervous talking about holiness, saints, and saintliness. Protestants are rightly concerned about the Roman Catholic view of saints on the one hand, and the Pentecostal view of holiness on the other. However, the subject is complex and when it comes up, the topic is usually quickly changed.

Still, saints are what we are and saints are what we are to become. This double meaning makes understanding sanctification very difficult. Ephesians 1:4 asserts that we have been chosen in Christ before the establishment of the world to be holy and blameless before God in love. Paul, writing to a group of Christians whom he will roundly criticize on a number of fronts, nevertheless addresses them as "those who are sanctified in Christ Jesus, called to be saints." (1 Cor. 1:2) That which is given is also commanded. Leviticus 19:2 reads: "You shall be holy, for I the LORD your God am holy." Belonging to God means that we are to be holy as God is holy. This text is repeated at 1 Peter 1:15–16. A few years ago American churches were rightly involved with peacemaking in fidelity to the biblical imperative: "pursue peace with everyone." (Heb. 12:14) However, the verse continues: "and (pursue) the holiness without which no one will see the Lord." God's command for us to be holy and our struggle to obey are serious matters, but sanctification does not stand alone as an impossible demand.

Justification and Sanctification

Chapters 7 and 9 belong together because God's pardon of sinners and our grateful response with our lives are dynamically or dialectically related. This conviction is near the heart of Reformed theology and was the main cause of the Protestant Reformation. Clearly differences of opinion persist between Roman Catholics and Protestants, and the issues remain rather complex and at times technical. Adopting the Protestant view, we argue that justification and sanctification are one in origin but two in experience. They are twin graces given from God and received by faith, which is also the gift of God. God's grace in and through Jesus Christ is therefore responsible for both justification and sanctification, which constitutes their unity. However, Christians experience them differently in that our justification is accomplished once-for-all by the work of Jesus Christ while our sanctification is being accomplished continually by the work of the Holy Spirit through our union with Christ.

According to Roman Catholic theology, justification and sanctification are the same. For Catholics, in some sense, justification is a continuous process and the human will is understood to have a cooperative function, suggesting that God does less and the human more. Protestants see this view of continuous justification as a confusion of justification and sanctification. Additionally, Protestants believe that the Roman Catholic doctrine of the human will in salvation "co-operating" with the "operating" God diminishes God's grace because it entails that salvation is not by grace alone but is the act together of God *and* the human. In this view God is not given the entire credit for our salvation because our striving remains an aspect of it.

Reformed theology, on the other hand, insists that when justification and sanctification are not kept properly distinct, God's once-for-all gift of faith (i.e. , salvation) and our continual struggle for holiness become confused. To begin with, the classical Protestant affirmation of the nature of justification is necessary to affirm, namely that in Jesus Christ God has once and for all forgiven us. This is our justification through the faith that is God's gift. However, we need to make a second point, to affirm that in Jesus Christ we must continually strive to live the holy life that we undertake with the advocacy and power of the Holy Spirit. The emphasis in justification is on what God has done for us in Jesus Christ. The emphasis in sanctification is on what we must do for God with the aid of God's Holy Spirit, although here too we emphasize that this striving also is in and through Jesus Christ.

Even though we are not its cause, God's forgiveness connects with us in our struggle for saintliness. No one of us deserves to be forgiven. Therefore Protestants believe Christians are justified (or made righteous) by God's grace alone. The finality of God's forgiveness issues in our own struggle for saintliness. Forgiveness and saintliness are both the work of God in and with us but in different ways. The need to relate faith and works is clearly demonstrated by two biblical citations. According to Romans we are justified by faith apart from works (3:28), while according to James, faith without works is dead (2:17). Christians believe both and in a practical way every Christian feels gratitude for the gift of faith (chapter 2) and responsible for the task of work, especially to obey the command to be holy, which is our present topic.

This righteousness, however, is *imputed* to us, not *imparted* to us. This distinction is important, though rather difficult to understand. Since forgiveness is imputed to us and not imparted to us, we are not really righteous in ourselves but only as we are united to Jesus Christ our Lord. He is our righteousness (1 Cor. 1:30) and apart from him we can do nothing (John 15:5). Some Christians believe the opposite, that God's forgiveness of our sins makes us "essentially" righteous. According to them, righteousness is *imparted* to us or *infused* into us by God's grace so that holiness becomes our nature and possession. Protestants reject the doctrine of "imparted grace" in favor of "imputed grace." Imparted grace means that Christ gives us grace so that our lives can proceed by themselves. According to Reformed theology, imparted grace represents the sin of pride. Imputed grace means that we are *declared* righteous because God's grace has united us with the only righteous one, Jesus Christ. We are not righteous in ourselves but only in him. God does not make us righteous by nature. God forgives our sin by grace. We live by grace.

The doctrine of our union with Christ tries to make clear the relationship between righteousness and grace. Our union with Christ means salvation does not "happen above us." The imputation of forgiveness, rather than its infusion, is designed to remind Christians that God's sovereign generosity to us is found in Jesus Christ and not in ourselves. In union with Christ we participate in that which is his alone, his righteousness before the Father. Christian behavior in theory and practice is treated in detail in theological ethics (a subject we hope to consider in a future work), but in doctrinal terms the Protestant Reformation affirmed justification by faith and denied sanctification by works in this way. Clearly the relation between God's act of forgiveness and our struggle toward saintliness still remains a complex matter, requiring careful reflection.

The Call to Holiness

The call to holiness, or saintliness, is a central imperative of Christian faith. The life of faith is a godly or holy life reflecting the holiness of God. The holy life in faith is both an indicative and an imperative. We are already holy because we are in union with Christ (the meaning of justification), and we are to become holy because that act is the true task of our lives (the meaning of sanctification). John Calvin and Karl Barth provide us reliable guidance. Calvin writes, "As long as Christ remains outside of us, and we are separated from him, all that he has suffered and done for the salvation of the human race remains useless and of no value to us." Calvin goes on to say that we are united to Christ by the bond of the Holy Spirit, effecting a union between Christ and ourselves, "a sacred wedlock through which we are made flesh of his flesh and bone of his bone (Eph. 5:30), and thus one with him" (*Inst.* III.1.3). The doctrine of union with Christ was discussed in chapter 2 in terms of faith. This doctrine is also the center of practical life for the Reformed Christian. Building directly on Calvin's insight, Karl Barth argues that our saintliness or sanctification "consists in the participation of the saints in the sanctity of Jesus Christ; in what Calvin called the *participatio Christi*."[1] In other words, our saintliness is, through our union with Christ by the power of the Holy Spirit, a sharing in Christ's holiness.

Thus, justification—defined as the once-for-all forgiveness of the elect in Jesus Christ—is a past, completed event. Sanctification, on the other hand, is defined as the continual struggle for saintliness although our striving is also part of God's work in us. Because of our union with Christ, we are obligated to live ever more faithfully into our communion with God. A human being experiences a natural birth as a creature, next comes a spiritual birth (born again or anew or from above) as a Christian when one becomes aware of God's forgiveness and the gift of new life, and then begins a lifelong struggle toward saintliness. The struggle to live as a saint is not the condition of our salvation (the Catholic view), but the struggle is certainly the consequence of our salvation (the Protestant view).

Unfortunately, the practice of saintliness is a struggle in which we often feel alone and helpless. Three conditions contribute to that result. First, some Christians think that forgiveness is what God does and that becoming holy is our task, but the good we want to do we cannot and do not do, and the evil that we do not want to do we still do (Rom. 7:19). We know we are trapped in our negative habits. Not only our flesh but also our wills are caught in the net of sin and evil, unable to resist the negative spirals that suck us downward into defeat and despair. A war rages within us, and when we are on the verge of doing good, evil lies close at hand (Rom. 7:21).

Second, we find little help from our primary community. Mainline churches provide low accountability at the level of personal, spiritual discipline. We struggle alone with the mandate to be holy. In respecting our privacy, our brothers and sisters in Christ are reluctant to impose demands and unwilling to hold us to spiritual accountability. The modern notion of voluntary church membership often involves understanding the church as a society of free association rather than a school for holiness that we must attend all our lives.

Third, the power of the Holy Spirit seems to many Christians an elusive and remote reality—not doubted but also not experienced. These people believe that the struggle for holiness depends entirely on them. With this type of thinking, the gospel mandate to become and be holy is experienced as a crushing burden and Christian life is fraught with terrible performance anxiety.

The mystery of God's declaration that in Christ we are already saints and yet we must strive to become saints requires, as we have seen, a distinction between the doctrines of justification and sanctification. On the one hand, when God justifies us we are passive. Forgiveness is done to us in Jesus Christ. On the other hand, when God sanctifies us we are expected to be active and accountable. At the same time the Holy Spirit is at work with us in the struggle toward saintliness.

The relation between justification and sanctification can be illustrated as follows. While family patterns are more complicated today, we can still recognize that we do not return to our parents' home in order to *become* their children. We were their children before we left the house and also when we return. Likewise our being forgiven by God is a status. However, because of our love and gratitude to our mothers and fathers, when we go home many of us look around for good and useful things to do to please them. We should think of the struggle for saintliness not as a condition of becoming a member of the family, but as a consequence of already being a member of it. In a real sense the requirements of the holy life are a list of things God our Father wants done around the house he created. These important tasks won't get done unless we make an effort. Being and acting go together.

In this approach, the grace is that Christ sends us the Holy Spirit to help us live the way the Father wants us to live. The demand for us to be holy should not be a burden since we do not carry it alone. That is, God's Holy Spirit is on and by our side in the struggle for saintliness. The apostle Paul tells us in 1 Corinthians 1:30 that Jesus Christ is our sanctification. Our Lord prays to the Father, "for their sakes I sanctify myself, so that they also may be sanctified in truth." (John 17:19) Christ is not separated from our being and becoming saints. Nevertheless, we must assume an active measure of responsibility for this task. We are not puppets of divine manipulation. In Christ, God renews our wills and delivers us from the vortex of sin so that we are no longer incapable and incompetent. We can and do work out our salvation in fear and trembling (Phil. 2:12), even though our work is by grace a response to our being united with Christ and empowered by the Holy Spirit. God's good work in and with us changes us so we can be faithful. Thus we experience saintliness both as gift given in grace and received by faith, and as a struggle in which we work very hard to cast off all that is not godly in our lives.

Clearly, then, to help us in this struggle we need an understanding of the role of God's Holy Son and Holy Spirit in the process of our being and becoming saints. We also need to develop a view of the church as an intentional, high-accountability fellowship that takes very seriously its nature as the Body of Christ. In other words, saintliness requires the Holy Son, the Holy Spirit, and the Holy Community.

The Struggle toward Holiness

The Holy Son

Jesus is only rarely described as "holy" in the New Testament. Yet the notion of Jesus as the Holy One of God permeates every page. In the Gospel according to Luke, the holiness of Jesus is related to his birth in words that ring with Christmas wonder and miracle. Responding to her confusion over the possibility of the birth of a son when she had as yet no husband, the angel says to Mary, "The Holy Spirit will come upon you, and the power of the Most High will overshadow you; therefore the child to be born will be holy; he will be called Son of God." (1:35) From the very beginning of his life, Jesus is holy, that is, godly. The nativity account also teaches that the proper theological emphasis is not on the virginity of Mary but on the action of the Holy Spirit. As the divine agent acting upon Mary at his conception and also at his baptism, the Holy Spirit comes upon Jesus (Luke 3:22). Jesus is recognized as "the Holy One of God" (Luke 4:34; also John 6:69) and three times in the Acts of the Apostles he is called the holy servant (or child) of God (3:13–14; 4:27, 30). Paul spoke of Jesus as the Son of God "with power according to the spirit of holiness." (Romans 1:4) In the Epistle to the Hebrews, the author wrote concerning Jesus that "it was fitting that we should have such a high priest, holy, blameless, undefiled, separated from sinners, and exalted above the heavens." (7:26)

Most Christians accept the holiness of Jesus, but many do not recognize the connection of the Lord's holiness with the holiness of the disciples. As the Holy One, Jesus offers his holiness to the church: "for their sakes I sanctify myself, so that they also may be sanctified in truth." (John 17:19) The holiness of Jesus is not for himself but given for the benefit of the church. The correct meaning is not that Jesus lived an ethically superior life in order that his disciples might do the same by imitation. Rather, our Lord, the Holy One of God (John

6.69), joins his disciples to himself as he declares at the end of the High Priestly prayer, "that the love with which you have loved me may be in them, and I in them." (John 17:26) Outside of our union with Christ, saintliness remains a forlorn struggle for us.

The Holy Spirit

The Christian life is the holy life as by grace and in the Holy Spirit we participate in the holiness of Jesus Christ. Christians are profoundly connected with the inner person and mission of Jesus himself that shapes every aspect of life, private and social, individual and communal. The work of the Holy Spirit applies the blessings of the gospel of Jesus Christ to each of us as personal participants in grace. This life in the Spirit is called in the Bible being "born again" and leads to the Christian life as our life "in Christ" as opposed to our life "in Adam." The Christian life begins not with us but with Jesus Christ. James S. Stewart once wrote that the

> heart of Paul's religion is union with Christ. This, more than any other conception—more than justification, more than sanctification, more even than reconciliation—is the key which unlocks the secrets of his soul. . . . If one seeks for the most characteristic sentences the apostle ever wrote, they will be found . . . where his intense intimacy with Christ comes to expression.[2]

When Paul writes, "To all the saints in Christ Jesus who are in Philippi" he means to the Christians in Philippi who are saints because they are "in Christ." Similarly, the initial blessing in Ephesians is "To the saints who are in Ephesus and are faithful in Christ Jesus." (1:1) The plural designation indicates that holiness as the mark of the Christian life applies both to a communion with Jesus and a communion among the saints.

Being "in Christ" defines not only a Christian's situation but also a Christian's way of life. Believers are expected to live "in Christ." Paul instructs Christians to "rejoice in the Lord." (Phil. 3:1) Tryphaena and Tryphosa "labor in the Lord." (Rom. 16:12) Christians trust (Phil. 2:14), stand fast (1 Thess. 3:8), are strong (Eph. 6:10), speak boldly

(Eph. 6:20), die (1 Cor. 15:18), know and are persuaded (Rom. 14:14), and hope (Phil. 2:19) in the Lord. These lived virtues, attitudes, and activities are representative expressions in daily life of the redemptive reality of the Christian's status "in Christ." Our salvation through and intimacy with Christ is lived out in concrete and practical ways as saintliness in action.

The Holy Community

Being members of the body of Christ refers not to mere sociability but the communion that characterizes Christian existence. Believers are corporately "in the Lord," and in him alone do they have community and unity. Galatians 3:28 states that Christians "are all one in Christ Jesus." "In him the whole structure (of the body of Christ) is joined together and grows into a holy temple in the Lord." (Eph. 2:21) The Thessalonians are gathered into one church that is "in God the Father and in the Lord Jesus Christ." (1:1) These texts do not teach that Christians are social animals bound together by bonds like common causes, similar experiences, and mutuality of need or even shared belief. Unity and community lie objectively in Jesus Christ and not subjectively in those things that we imagine we have in common.

The Christian is not "in Christ" alone but is bound with others in a communion of love as the body of Christ. Membership in the church is not a personal decision to join a fellowship but a calling to worship and service in Christ. In the New Testament Jesus Christ exists only in the singular, but saints exist in the plural. No solitary saints are present in the New Testament. Saintliness is clearly tied in with what it means to live as the community of the faithful. Further, Protestants have also believed, perhaps surprisingly for some readers, that we could not have God as our Father, and Christ as our savior, without the Church as our Mother. According to Calvin, for those to whom God is Father the church will also be Mother (*Inst.* IV.1.1). The reformer could refer clearly to Mother Church—the visible, historical Church—as the community that nurtures Christian birth and growth and argue that the mothering qualities of the Church are necessary for salvation (*Inst.* IV.1.4). Christian formation means Christians drinking from their own wells, within their own communities of faith.

Being Born Again *and Again*

The claim to be a "born-again Christian" is widely heard in the United States. The term is used emphatically and often challengingly. Sometimes the phrase seems to be judgmental, making a distinction between genuine and nominal Christians. Sometimes the term appears descriptive, like the distinction between liberal and conservative Christians. Occasionally the phrase seems historic, like the division between Catholic and Protestant Christians. Given the variety of usage, "born-again Christian" usually includes the notion of human choice in salvation and excludes a view of divine election by grace alone. In addition, "born again" nearly always indicates some kind of sudden "conversion experience," which is regarded as an essential element in true Christianity. Knowledge of this conversion experience often includes a specific date and place where it occurred.

In the King James version of the Bible (1611), Jesus says to Nicodemus, "You must be born again." (John 3:7) However the Revised Standard Version (1946) reads, "You must be born anew" and notes that the verse could equally well be translated, "You must be born from above." These statements indicate that every Christian without exception must be "born again" or "born anew" or "born from above." Regeneration therefore applies to all Christians. Being born anew is a relatively neutral manner of speaking, but being born from above clearly indicates that the rebirth that makes a Christian is the work of divine grace. The term "born again" standing alone might be understood as "you must choose to be born again," with only one legitimate form of the experience allowed. We prefer a broader rendering, one that we suggest is Biblical. Christians are taught they must be regenerated from above by God's grace. This act is God's doing and is not reducible to any one form of experience.

No Christian surely denies human accountability and responsibility, but salvation is a gift of God before being chosen by us. The popular term "born again" reminds us of the mystery in the relation between the finality of God's forgiveness and our struggle for saintliness. That is, Christians are born from above by God's grace (justification). They are also born anew every day through the work of the Holy Spirit (sanctification). In short, Christians are all "born again." They are also born again and again and again.

To summarize, all is grace, for Jesus Christ is our justification and our sanctification (1 Cor. 1:30); yet we also must heed the call, "sleeper, awake!" (Eph. 5:14) In union with Christ, the Holy One of God, Christians arise from slumber to struggle for holiness in obedience to God to live lives of faithfulness to the glory of God. God demands our living the amended life as Christians because in Jesus Christ we are already saints of God.

10

The Accident of Sin

In public worship over the years I have regularly offered the assurance of pardon in Christ's name to the community of the faithful. However, a public absolution, which is part of the expected liturgy, provides the protection of the ministerial office in a corporate setting. But sitting in a small room and looking directly into another person's eyes and hearing the story of sin's effect in lost creativity and joy in Christian service is more personal and therefore exposed and vulnerable. Only once in my forty years as a pastor have I felt authorized to pronounce God's forgiveness directly to a single person. I believed that the terrible consequences of sin in its capacity to undermine God's purposes for a person's life required absolution. Two people were directly involved, and issues such as arrogance, repentance, abuse, and acceptance were swirling around two human heads and hearts.

Grateful to God for the call to pastoral ministry, I have nevertheless been terrified of trifling with God's great mysteries, being all too aware of my own lack of spiritual insight. I believe in absolution from sins and assurance of pardon based on Matthew 6:14 ("For if you forgive others their trespasses, your heavenly Father will also forgive you") and Matthew 16:19 ("I will give you the keys of the kingdom of heaven, and whatever you bind on earth will be bound in heaven, and whatever you loose on earth will be loosed in heaven"). Still, the assurance of pardon is an awesome power for God to give and an even more fearsome responsibility for any pastor to claim and apply directly.

We were simply having a quiet discussion when to my amazement the conversation turned intensely intimate and painful, and as I listened I came to the astonished conclusion that I was hearing an indirect but real confession of sin. In itself such events are not unusual. Every minister is familiar with sad, tragic, and secret stories, and we are always sympathetic and offer what comfort we can. I was convinced that this situation required more than sympathy and comfort. Later, at home, I became aware that the events had been told to me so many years after they had occurred because I was to be God's instrument of absolution. Sin long past was confounding the present and the future life of one from whom God was calling forth an important ministry for the church. This realization was a terrible conviction for me, and the responsibility to accomplish this once-in-a-ministerial-lifetime assignment of individual absolution and assurance of pardon came upon me with a force that I could neither avoid nor evade. I telephoned early the next morning and insisted upon an appointment.

My final act was to request the use of this wonderful prayer every day for a week.

> O God our Father, we who are children of time come to thee who art above time. For us the days that are past are past beyond recall and what we have written on life's page we may not erase. But our past is still present to thee and thou canst undo what is beyond our power to change. Thou canst restore the wasted years. And we bring them to thee—all the time past of our lives. Take it into thy moulding hands. What was amiss, do thou amend. What was faulty do thou fulfill. We bless thee for forgiveness but we ask for more, even that thou shouldst annul the evil that we have done and accomplish the good in which we failed. We thank thee that thou art ever open to our cry, that none can come to thee too late, that the door of the Father's house is never closed to any child who would come home. Father, we come bringing our marred lives for thy remaking, our stained hands for thy cleansing, our tired feet for thy rest, our wearied hearts for thy peace.
>
> Robert E. Speer

I can think of many objections to this prayer, but surely we may hope that God's mercy is quite beyond our calculations. That God would annul the evil we have done and accomplish the good we failed to do is the cry of every sensitive heart. I do not know the effect of this prayer nor the rest of the story. They belong to God and another

Christian life—not mine. The point is that the gospel is about God's grace countering sin, creating new life out of the deadliness of the old, and the empowerment for freedom for the future.

The Origin of Sin

Nearly every human being recognizes the reality of evil, and one expects that most Christians accept sin as a pervasive fact of life. Accounting for sin and evil is not so obvious, however. The concept of sin against God is often set within the larger context of the problem or mystery of evil in the world. The word "problem" is generally used if some hope is present that the question can be resolved. The word "mystery" is employed if no hope of solution is considered possible. The conclusion we adopt here is that evil and sin are finally inexplicable. The proper strategy for Christians is not to find a reasonable explanation of sin but to live in the faith that God overcomes it.

The most popular outline of Christian theology consists of three points:

1. God created everything good.
2. Men and women abused the good gift of free will, thereby falling into sin.
3. In response to sin, God sent Jesus Christ to redeem the world.

According to this understanding, sin is the pivotal event between creation and redemption that requires (and explains) the incarnation. Sin is set before grace, as if it were understandable on its own terms.

An additional problem concerns free will. Why would an omnipotent, omniscient, all-good God create so devastating a capacity as human free will, which has led to such unmitigated horror? Thinkers have struggled for centuries to hold together an understanding of God's power, God's goodness, and the existence of evil. For example, the Greek philosopher Epicurus, some three hundred years before Christ, asked, "Is God willing to prevent evil, but not able? Then God is not all-powerful. Is God able to prevent evil, but not willing? Then God is not all-good. If God is both willing and able to prevent evil, from whence does evil come?" This question could be answered by denying the reality of evil, or by denying the omnipotence of God, or by denying that God is all good. In refusing those options theologians have usually fallen back on 'free will.' This defense holds that even God could not create free creatures without providing bad and even deadly choices for them. The difficulty with this solution is that it denies God's omnipotence. If recognizably free choices exist between good things, like apples and oranges, why must humans have the choice to eat arsenic? We need not pursue these difficult philosophical issues further here, for equally difficult theological concerns demand our attention.

Some Christians consider themselves to be "supralapsarian" and others claim to be "infralapsarian" (or sublapsarian). Both terms contain the word 'lapsed,' referring to the Fall. The supralapsarians believe that salvation comes *before* the Fall and infralapsarians hold that salvation occurs *after* the Fall. Infralapsarians believe that salvation is a response to sin, while supralapsarians believe that the Fall is part of God's original plan. In other words, for supralapsarians

1. God decrees grace and salvation to some and predestines others to justice and reprobation;
2. then God creates the world with the elect and reprobate in it, and;
3. then God permits the Fall.

For infralapsarians

1. God creates the whole world;
2. then God permits the Fall, and;
3. then God chooses to elect some to salvation.

The same unexamined assumption lies behind both of these views: sin must have a rational place in divine and human history. Understandably, we do not want to claim that sin came as a surprise to God, so some people opine that sin was foreordained by God and others insist that sin is only foreknown by God. However, on either view more questions are raised than answered. Even when the terms supra- and infralapsarian are explained, most Christians cannot choose between them, because while sin is a fact, no one can satisfactorily account for sin's existence in a world where a loving God created everything.

Obviously, sin that is inexplicable cannot be explained. Complicated theological discussions that try to explain what is beyond explanation are counterproductive. Christians cannot explain the origin of evil and the existence of sin, and they should not try.

The Extent of Sin

The Westminster Shorter Catechism provides the well-known definition of sin as "any want of conformity unto, or transgression of, the Law of God." (Answer 14) Since sin is the object of the wrath of God and produces our death (Rom. 6:23), the subject would seem to be impossible to take too seriously. Our sin estranges us from God and each other, and the result is condemnation. Moreover, our human fascination with sin and evil is itself sinful and evil. We eagerly read newspapers and watch television full of tragedies and people who cause them. Evil literary figures like Shakespeare's Iago and Milton's Satan and evil historical figures like Adolf Hitler continue to hold our interest.

According to popular culture, Reformed theology is identified with a view of sin called "total depravity." "Calvinism" is often used as a synonym for the gloomiest possible evaluation of the human condition and its most dreary prospects. However, does the doctrine of "total depravity" properly explain the scriptural assertion that all have sinned and fallen short of the glory of God (Rom. 3:23)? Most Christians are willing to accept that men and women are sometimes weak and ignorant and make serious mistakes, but for some the notion of total depravity is too gloomy to serve as an accurate description of the human condition. Roman Catholic theology with its doctrine of co-operating grace and the Wesleyan view of Christian perfection are examples of the denial of total depravity. Catholics assume that we are still good enough to work alongside God, as it were, in pursuit with God of our salvation. John Wesley rejected article 15 of the Thirty-Nine Articles of the Church of England where Christ alone is declared sinless. Wesley thought humans could also be sinless because they were not totally depraved. In other words, Wesley considered human sinlessness our greatest goal. In contrast, John Calvin considered human sinlessness our greatest presumption and therefore a profoundly sinful aspiration. According to Calvin, Christians are sinless only in Christ but not at all in themselves.

Total depravity in Reformed theology does not mean that all are as bad as they could possibly be. Quite evidently we could all be worse. Further, total depravity does not mean that the human condition is totally without good. Many things about human life can be rightly praised. Total depravity means that nothing about us is beyond the reach of sin. Most Christians are willing to ask God's forgiveness for their evil deeds, but Reformed Christians also ask God to forgive their good deeds because they believe sin can lurk in those things for which all the world praises us. This conviction is a necessary implication of the fact that our confidence is founded on faith in Jesus Christ alone and not at all in ourselves or our works—even in our good works. Reformed theology is careful to deny the temptation to take some satisfaction and even expect to derive some credit before God for the good we do because to God alone is the glory given.

Divine Grace and Human Sin

Reformed theology takes sin seriously indeed. However, Reformed theology takes even more seriously the theological order by which we understand the relation of human sin to God's grace. God's grace precedes human sin. Discussing sin as a subject by itself (as in this chapter) distorts the gospel unless sin is considered in the context of God's prior grace. Nevertheless, within the context of God's grace, nothing human is beyond the reach of sin. In that sense human depravity is total. Reformed theology, then, does not begin with 'total depravity' but with the forgiving, loving, reconciling grace of God. The unfortunate conclusion that theology begins with sin may be inferred from the popular acronym that is often used as a summary of Reformed theology. The letters of TULIP are used to teach

Total depravity
Unconditional election
Limited atonement
I rresistible grace
Perseverance (or Preservation) of the saints

The chief problem is not the doctrines selected as definitive for Reformed theology, but the order of their presentation. For all its cleverness as an aid to memory, the TULIP sequence distorts

Reformed theology. The critical point is that Christian theology properly begins with divine grace, not human sin. God's unmerited favor to us precedes our recognition of sin. The result of beginning theological reflection with total depravity is the tragic loss of the sheer and utter glory of God's grace in Jesus Christ and its replacement by a dismal and often unhealthy view of human being.

The Clouds of Unknowing

We cannot provide reasons for the existence of sin and evil in God's world. The fact of sin must be taken with absolute seriousness, however impossible to state its meaning. Sin is a fact with horrible consequences, but as a fact sin is finally inexplicable. This conclusion follows an insight of John Calvin who defined sin as "adventitious" (*Inst.* II.1.11), which means that theology provides no acceptable explanation of the existence of evil in a world that Christians believe was created and is governed by the all-powerful and all-good God. To say sin is *accidental* means it is incomprehensible and would not be sin if it were full of meaning. Sin exists, but Christians cannot affirm that God has a purpose for it. In other words, sin is a terrible reality but not a meaningful category for theological reflection on its purported purpose.

Since we recognize the reality of sin but cannot explain its origin or existence, the result is a proper humility before God and a healthy skepticism toward each other. Reformed Christians especially accept the truth of the Latin phrase *simul justus, simul peccatur*: the saint is also a sinner. Even the most righteous cause is still served by sinners. Anyone who comes to believe that her cause or his person is exempt from the reach of corruption has lost the virtue of skeptical detachment and spiritual realism that Reformed Christians have built into the heart of their theology. The Reformed doctrine of total depravity is a salutary and necessary reminder of our human limitations. Obviously, evil should be opposed and restrained, but the ends toward which good people strive and the means that they use must also be constantly reexamined. A halo can become a noose! Even good people need to be constantly watched because the deceptions we practice on ourselves and on each other offer a dreary tale of thieves within and suckers without.

Many people think less of themselves than they ought to. Therefore a good deal of psychological and theological effort is rightly
directed toward making such folk accept what they are and can
become. However, many people think more highly of themselves than
they ought to. A wonderful literary illustration of this situation occurs
in Shakespeare's comedy *Love's Labor's Lost*, in which four young
noblemen take themselves entirely too seriously. They so forget the
theology of human limitations that they make a mighty vow to devote
three years of their lives consistently and completely to scholarly pur-
suits. However, to their intense surprise and chagrin, they soon find
their academic concentration quite shattered by the appearance of
four attractive young women. Since this play is a comedy and not a
tragedy, each man falls in love with a different woman and vice versa.
Now the men no longer desire to keep their vow, but they also do not
want to admit they were silly to make it in the first place. In their calculations the high-minded young men had not allowed for the obvious fact that women are a lot more interesting than books and they are
astonished to discover:

> For where is any author in the world
> Teaches such beauty as a woman's eye?
> A lover's eye will gaze an eagle blind
> A lover's ear will hear the lowest sound.
> From women's eyes this doctrine I derive
> They are the books, the arts, the academes
> That show, contain, and nourish all the world.
> (*Love's Labor's Lost*, IV.3. 312–13, 334–35, 350, 352–53)

The point Shakespeare is making in this play is that absolute confidence in any human condition or endeavor—including one's own
fidelity to an ideal—is so misplaced as to be comic, and such confidence can become tragic. Even our finest ideals are not beyond corruption because of the frailty to which flesh is heir.

The Greek philosopher Plato identified and recommended an
important and noble human aspiration when he taught that the goal
of life is the love of the perfect and best. To strive to live up to our
ideals is right and good, but Christians must never forget that if ide-
alists got what they deserve none of us would escape whipping. Skepticism is an accurate assessment of the human condition, and to ignore
skepticism is to court disaster. H. L. Mencken captured part of this

idea when he said, "Believing the worst about another person may be a sin, but it is seldom a mistake." The Reformed system of checks and balances is a reflection of the conviction (famously expressed by Lord Acton) that power corrupts and absolute power corrupts absolutely. For that reason church order in the Reformed tradition produced a representative democracy two hundred years before the American Republic was founded, thanks to the Scots!

The concept of sin as total depravity is not an unusual idea. Many, if not most, people are quite willing to apply it to their opponents. Reformed Christians are unusual in that they insist on applying the idea of total depravity to themselves. For them, no aspect of human life is exempt from the possibility of sin. At the same time, the recognition of our misery must not be used to dispraise God our Creator. We experience the fact of sin. The origin and meaning of sin are beyond our comprehension. The result of this situation is not pessimism but humility. The doctrine of total depravity, properly understood, is rather cheerful. Martin Luther, whose own frantic search for a forgiving God launched the Protestant Reformation, once advised his too-scrupulous friend, Philip Melanchthon, to "sin boldly." Christians are not allowed to sin in order that grace may abound (Rom. 6:1), but we are powerfully taught by the unexplainable reality of sin that we must humbly put our entire trust in God—whose love is revealed in Jesus Christ—and not at all in our own merits, which means we can and must accept the fact that we are forgiven.

11

The Comfort of Predestination

My parents are buried a thousand miles from where I now live. Whenever I am in that part of the country I always visit their graves to sit quietly for a few minutes, remembering and thanking God for them. Before leaving I walk around a bit because cemeteries are for remembering how precious life is. Recognizing the names of those who are no longer with us is sad, but I am grateful to so many who made a contribution to my life, if only a kind word spoken so long ago and cherished all these years. Reflecting on the full and happy lives of people like my mother and father is especially pleasant. At one tombstone near my parents I always pause and read again:

Lt. Clyde T. Dailey
January 15, 1917–February 1944
Went down with his plane
off the coast of Holland
The North Sea is Clyde's resting place
until the Great Pilot calls his airmen home.

I still remember Clyde and the big boys who became men very quickly and went across the ocean to fight for our freedom. Clyde was one of many men who fell into the restless sea and never came back to the home and the town and the life he protected and the woman he loved. Clyde's tombstone always throws me into the deepest reflection on the Christian view of God's providence and predestination. I leave the cemetery with both a passionate hope and a passionate conviction that these doctrines are true.

Christians are comforted by the belief that in prosperity and in adversity God is for us, in us, and with us. This conviction is not a deduction to be demonstrated to a skeptic but a mystery to be experienced by the faithful. The doctrine of God's providence is a theological affirmation of God's care for the world and everything in it. The doctrine of predestination is the special application of this conviction to God's care of the company of the faithful and the individual members of it.

An Ancient Problem

In one form or another, God's relation to what happens in the world is a very old problem. In the classical world the Epicureans championed the idea that the world was ruled by chance or fortune. They believed that things happened in unpredictable ways without reasons or causes, and therefore both happy and sad results were due to "luck." In contrast, the Stoics believed everything that happened was determined by necessity and therefore occurred by fate. This fatalistic view is represented in Hamlet's lines, "There's a divinity that shapes our ends, / Rough-hew them how we will" (V.2.10–11). To this notion is often added the idea that the gods are indifferent, or even malicious, toward human concerns. In *King Lear* Gloucester says, "As flies to wanton boys are we to the gods, / They kill us for their sport" (IV.1.38–39). The same idea is expressed in this story of an appointment in Samarra, which we paraphrase.

> Once upon a time a merchant in Baghdad sent his servant to the marketplace and he came back terrified. "Master," he said, "in the marketplace I bumped into Death, who made a threatening gesture toward me. I must get away from Baghdad so I can escape Death. I will ride to Samarra and Death will not find me." Borrowing a horse, the servant rode away as fast as he could. The merchant went to the marketplace and finding Death standing there asked why a threatening gesture had been directed toward his servant. Death said, "I did not make a gesture of threat but only of surprise. I did not expect to see your servant in Baghdad today because I have an appointment with him in Samarra tonight."[1]

The ancient world provided an intellectual choice between the Epicurean view that the world is neither designed nor governed and the Stoic view that everything in the world is inexorably determined. According to the Stoics, free will is an illusion since every effect has a fixed cause (Fate). However, the Stoics were not entirely consistent since they thought providence or fate applied only to big things and not to little ones. Against this view Christians insist God's providence extends to all things great and small. The philosophical debate between chance and necessity, fortune and fate has never been resolved. Apparently some Christian soldiers accepted the fatalistic view that "I cannot die until the bullet with my name on it is fired." This notion may have provided courage and comfort, but most Christians accept both divine sovereignty and human responsibility, meaning that God governs our lives but we are also responsible for them. These two affirmations require considerable reflection.

The Christian Answer

The Christian doctrine of providence, which affirms God's care for everything, and the doctrine of predestination, which affirms God's special care for every person, occupy an intermediate position between Epicurean chance and Stoic fate. Reformed theology especially claims that God, revealed to us in Jesus Christ, is in control of the world so that nothing occurs by fixed necessity or whimsical chance. The idea that God governs the world and everything in it is not easy to understand. For example, 2 Thessalonians teaches "God chose you from the beginning to be saved" (2:13) and the Gospel of John, "You did not choose me, but I chose you." (15:16) In these verses salvation is determined by God's choice. Likewise the apostle Paul wrote, God "chose us in him before the foundation of the world, that we should be holy and blameless before him." (Eph. 1:4) On the other hand, the scripture also appeals to human choice in verses like "if you be unwilling to serve the LORD, choose this day whom you will serve" (Josh. 24:15) or "the kingdom of God is at hand; repent, and believe in the Gospel. (Mark 1:15) The relation between divine and human choice is the question.

The doctrine of predestination confesses that in God's great love God chooses those who will be saved by grace. Salvation as anyone's "destination" is an act of God. God is the author of salvation but the details of *how* salvation is accomplished is God's secret. As a matter of God's grace more to be confessed than understood, predestination presents difficult issues. For example, most Christians believe that sin means that no one is ever worthy of being elect. Therefore only a few thinkers assert that God chooses to save those whose relative merit is foreseen or foreknown. Rather, God chooses the elect not because of any worthiness on their part but by God's grace alone. This view raises the objection that for God to choose some and reject others before they have done anything is arbitrary and unfair. Still, verses like Romans 9:18 teach "So then [God] has mercy upon whomever he wills, and he hardens the heart of whomever he wills."

Some Christians imagine the story can be told this way: God builds a large supermarket (God's creation) and arranging the various shelves as attractively as possible, God leaves us alone and goes to the check-out counter to wait (God's judgment). Being unattended (human free will) we can wander up and down the aisles and make choices as we desire. If we choose the package of faith, we are saved. If we choose unbelief, we are not saved. Other Christians, including those in the Reformed tradition, imagine that because we are children of God we are never left unattended in the store. Our Father always walks beside us. While in some sense the shopping cart is ours and we can choose from the lower shelves, some goods (like salvation) are beyond our reach. However, God created these goods for us, and therefore God puts them in the cart for us.

According to the first view God sets the context of human life, but salvation requires a human choice. The second view maintains that salvation is a divine choice that elicits a human response. In each case, the divine actions come first and the human reactions second but with varying understandings of the roles of divine sovereignty and human free will. The elect rejoice that their cart is filled with good things, but they rejoice even more that God accompanies them every step of the way from the store entrance (our physical conception) to the exit (our physical death). In the meanwhile our desires (see chapter 12 on prayer) constantly interact with God's will. God not only provides the *general* provisioning (providence) of the supermarket but also the *special* help (predestination) that each customer needs.

One reason for accepting a strong view of human free will is to avoid making God responsible for choosing both the elect (people who are saved) and the nonelect or reprobate (people who are not saved). However, this answer questions God's sovereign grace in salvation because salvation depends to some extent on human choice. Christians recognize some people are in the store whose carts appear to be empty. Moreover the scripture does teach that some people are nonelect or reprobate. However, we must remember the identity of the reprobate is known only to God. We are not free to determine in a certain and final way whose cart is and will remain empty. Humans are doubtless free to choose some things on the lower shelves, but the higher things, including the gift of salvation, depend on the Father's initiative. Therefore, Reformed Christians are obligated to treat all people with kindness and to hope that the Father will fill the carts of others as he has filled ours.

The Reformed Emphasis

Reformed theology has always taken with utmost seriousness the idea that we are enabled to love God because God first loved us (1 John 4:10). Unfortunately people sometimes forget that predestination is about God's love and not God's power. The doctrine of predestination as God's special providence for individuals who receive the gift of faith is widely accepted in Reformed theology and warmly denied in other traditions. The churches influenced by John Wesley, for example, are especially vigorous in rejecting predestination. However, all Christian theologies have some view of God's election since scripture teaches that God chose us in Jesus Christ before the foundation of the world that we should be holy and blameless before him in love (Eph. 1:4). The relations between chance and necessity, between human freedom and divine governance, are finally mysterious. Therefore, no interpretation of predestination can answer all legitimate questions. The emphasis is nevertheless clear. According to Reformed theology, Christian groups that reject predestination diminish God's sovereignty in the governance of the world by exalting human free will. Those who accept predestination by exalting God's sovereignty may be charged with diminishing the range of human freedom to choose.

Still, Reformed theology holds that confessing salvation by God's grace alone requires affirming the mystery of predestination. Even within the Reformed tradition, the doctrine of eternal election is seriously questioned by some people and others seem to be acutely embarrassed by their historic association with it. Predestination is both a rock on which some Christians have built their house and a stone that has caused others to stumble. Here, three issues should be mentioned: (1) the relation between logic and mystery, (2) the importance of confessional context, and (3) predestination as a believers' doctrine.

1. *The relation between logic and mystery.* Some Reformed theologians defend the doctrine of predestination as a logical implication of the complete sovereignty of God. They argue that since God's sovereignty includes omnipotence and omniscience, everything that happens is God's will. This view of "whatever will be, will be" appears identical with the Stoic doctrine. Additionally, acknowledging predestination provides a reasonable explanation of what happens in the world by tracing every event to God's will. The primary objection to this view is the underlying notion that God is the author of evil.

In contrast, predestination is not properly understood as a logical deduction based on God's sovereignty, but a humble conviction based on God's love revealed in Jesus Christ. Reformed Christians put a heavy emphasis on the conviction that God has the whole world in his hands. However, no theology can explain everything in the whole world, most notably sin and evil, as we saw in the previous chapter. Even the Westminster Confession, which only uses the word "mystery" one time, applies it to predestination (chapter 3, article 8). The conclusion is that the doctrines of providence and predestination clearly require the acceptance and confession of mystery.

2. *The importance of confessional context.* Predestination is a mystery. No human being knows the exact relation between God's love for the elect and God's election of the loved. Nevertheless, confessing the doctrine in the proper context is crucial. This point is demonstrated in the contrast between the Westminster Confession and John Calvin's writings. The Westminster Confession of 1644 is probably the most influential interpretation of Reformed theology in the English-speaking world. This confession deals with scripture in chapter 1, with God in chapter 2, and with election in chapter 3. This order of discussion suggests that in Westminster the doctrine of predestination is an attempt to explain from God's perspective the eternal choice of those whom God will love.

In contrast, in the final version of his masterwork, *The Institutes of the Christian Religion*, Calvin deals in Book I with the knowledge of God the Creator, that is, with God's creation of all things and God's providence for them. In Book II Calvin discusses the knowledge of God the Redeemer: the revelation in the Old and New Testaments; the two natures and one person of the mediator and his three offices (prophet, king, and priest). In Book III Calvin expounds the work of the Holy Spirit: the gift of faith (his longest chapter) and the double grace of regeneration (sanctification) and justification, and also prayer (the second longest chapter). Only then does Calvin develop the doctrine of eternal election (predestination). Book IV is devoted to the church, its officers, sacraments, and civil government. The point is that predestination for Calvin is the concluding section of the doctrine of salvation (soteriology). Predestination is not developed in Book I in terms of the doctrine of God (theology proper), nor in Book II of the Redeemer (Christology), but at the end of Book III as part of the understanding of humanity. Clearly Calvin expounds upon many doctrines before treating predestination, a fact that makes extremely difficult the claim that predestination is Calvin's "central dogma." For Calvin predestination is the believer's humble attempt to understand the miracle of faith. In the Westminster Confession predestination is an attempt to look over God's shoulder toward creation and redemption. In Calvin's work, predestination is seen over the believer's shoulder looking toward God's grace.

3. *Predestination as a believers' doctrine*. Predestination in Reformed theology is properly a believers' doctrine expressing the experience of the miracle of God's love revealed to faith. Most Christians gladly, if somewhat vaguely, affirm the Father's care of his children, including the conviction that salvation comes entirely from God. However, the question about people without faith, the nonelect or reprobate, inevitably arises. One response to the issue of the nonelect is to deny predestination and insist that salvation is entirely or partially a matter of human choice. Another option is to accept *single* predestination, which means that election is affirmed but reprobation is entirely ignored or denied. Reformed theology has normally maintained *double* predestination, maintaining that God's will governs both election and reprobation. If God elects some people, then those whom God does not elect are reprobate. The scripture teaches that salvation comes through faith, which is a gift of God. That some people do not

have the gift of faith is usually explained as both God's will and also as somehow the individual's choice and fault.

The conclusion is that God's election is a mystery that believers experience but cannot explain. The nonelect is a biblical category, but no Christian is allowed to speculate or try to determine who belongs to it. All people must from a practical standpoint be treated as potentially elect. John Calvin, citing Augustine, wrote, "'For as we know not who belongs to the number of the predestined or who does not belong, we ought to be so minded as to wish that all men be saved.' So shall it come about that we try to make everyone we meet a sharer in our peace." (*Inst.* III.23.14)

The discussion of predestination can be introduced this way. Some years ago the church we attended celebrated the Maundy Thursday Communion service by having husband-and-wife teams distribute the bread and wine. The couple sitting next to us had invited their son to the service, but he chose instead to go out with a friend. His parents never saw him alive again. Scott was killed in a terrible automobile accident that snowy night. Apparently he and his friend had been drinking and the friend was driving too fast. He lost control of the car and hit a steel bridge abutment, killing Scott and severely injuring the driver. Scott was just a few weeks from completing college and had splendid prospects for the future. His death plunged the family and indeed the whole congregation into deep mourning.

In struggling with such issues, John Calvin suggests three kinds of will in every situation: a human will, an evil will, and the divine will. (*Inst.* I.4.2) The decision to go out with a friend is an example of human free will. The failure to negotiate a curve during a heavy snow is an example of the evil that can occur. Clearly the natural conditions that surround human beings and the results of their decisions and failures sometimes lead to error and can be magnified into tragedy. In our regret for the former and our grief for the latter, Christians are not different from other people. However, Christians also believe that God is with us in our decisions and in our tragedies and to God belongs the victory in which we participate because of our union with Christ. To Reformed Christians the doctrine of predestination asserts the divine love toward God's faithful people, which affirms the ultimate victory of God's sovereignty and holy will to bestow grace upon us.

12

The Miracle of Prayer

Toward the end of my first month as a newly ordained minister, I learned that the sixteen-year-old son of two parishioners had been killed only a few weeks before I had arrived at the church. I was told by others that a group of young people were returning from a summer swim in a nearby lake when their car, which had been traveling at an excessive speed, skidded at a sharp curve in the road and rolled over and over with such force that three of the four doors were ripped off and Jimmy was thrown from the car. One of the girls was bounced from the back seat into the front seat but, except for Jimmy, no one else was seriously injured. Somehow in the violent expulsion Jimmy's lung was punctured. That evening, people in the small town (including the bruised teenagers who were in the accident) met to pray that Jimmy's life be spared. In spite of everyone's efforts, the bleeding could not be stopped, and the next day Jimmy died. Jimmy died because one of the girls in the car had recently "broken up" with the young man who chose that afternoon to express his anger by driving a car dangerously fast. A few days later this driver served as a pallbearer at the funeral of his friend whose death he had accidentally caused.

In the years I was their pastor Jimmy's parents never indicated a desire to talk about this tragedy. I felt obliged to respect their unwillingness to discuss their grief with me or even to reveal except very indirectly the pain of unanswered prayer. This situation taught me in a powerful way that ordinary people carry great tragedies in their lives that they do not share with others. Every pastor can predict the presence of at least one broken heart in every home in the parish. According to Job 5:7 the human race is born to trouble as the sparks fly upward. Of course Christians trust in God's ultimate victory over all troubles, but life is nonetheless full of tragedy. For most Christians one of the first responses to tragedy is prayer which asks for benefits that God is able to bestow, but prayer also includes a petition to bear the denial of our requests.

Prayer can be defined as God's miraculous willingness to include answering our joys and concerns in the government of the world. God's willingness is made possible by God's omnipotence and motivated by God's love for us. Prayer should be regarded as an awesome mystery because it is a miracle that God listens and responds to us. According to John Calvin, prayer is the chief exercise of faith,[1] which means that because of our union with Christ we are able in spite of our sinfulness to approach God with genuine confidence and make our requests known. That God hears and heeds our prayers is a wonderful promise of the triune God. Prayer requires faith, which is the gift of the Holy Spirit. Moreover, by the advocacy of the Holy Spirit, believers pray to the loving Father who is revealed in Jesus Christ.

The reality of prayer is, of course, best experienced in its actual practice rather than in its theoretical conception. Since prayer as an activity is more important than the construction of a doctrine of prayer, most writing about prayer is really instruction in its practice (often following the outline of the Lord's Prayer in Matt. 6:9–13). However, correct behavior and correct belief go together. The practice of prayer usually proceeds in confidence, but the theory of prayer often encounters difficulties. The expected result of this doctrinal discussion of prayer is that Christians will pray with more joy and greater reverence when the miraculousness of prayer is recognized.

To skeptics, prayer is a futile exercise. According to them God's governance of the universe does not require information from us about our needs or advice on how to deal with them. The philosopher Immanuel Kant considered prayer an activity that a reasonable person would be ashamed to be caught performing. However, philosophers are not the only group to disdain prayer. On occasion some prominent Christian asserts rather defiantly that he no longer prays. For example, in a recasting of Christian doctrine that caused a furor at the time, the Anglican Bishop John A. T. Robinson wrote in *Honest to God* of a remembered relief from twenty years past in finding "a kindred spirit, to whom also the whole of the teaching we received on prayer (as it happened to be in this case) meant equally little."[2] In a chapter on "worldly holiness" Robinson presents "A 'Non-religious' Understanding of Prayer," which is defined not as address to God but "openness to the ground of our being." Presumably the claim that one no longer addresses God in prayer indicates emancipation from a "childish" and "irrational" practice. In reality denying prayer is one of the most telling evidences of loss of faith. Or, as Calvin puts it, "[T]he true test of faith lies in prayer."[3]

Two Difficulties

Two important issues concerning prayer must be mentioned. First is the intellectual difficulty focused around the prayer of petition or request. Second is the psychological difficulty of understanding the role of our sin in our prayer.

For some thinkers the prayers of adoration, confession, and thanksgiving do not conflict with God's governance of the world since their purpose is to make human beings more reverent, more humble, and more grateful. According to the skeptical Voltaire, the only fitting prayer is that of submission.[4] In contrast, the prayer of petition asks God to do something. Other kinds of prayer change us, but the prayer of request intends to change God's will or change something in the world. The American humorist Mark Twain illustrates this approach to prayer in his satirical account of Huck Finn's request for fish hooks.

> Miss Watson she took me in the closet and prayed, but nothing come of it. She told me to pray every day, and whatever I asked for I would get it. But it warn't so. I tried it. Once I got a fish-line, but no hooks. It warn't any good to me without hooks. I tried for the hooks three or four times, but somehow I couldn't make it work. By and by, one day, I asked Miss Watson to try for me, but she said I was a fool. She never told me why, and I couldn't make it out no way. I set down one time back in the woods, and had a long think about it. I says to myself, if a body can get anything they pray for, why don't Deacon Winn get back the money he lost on pork? . . . No, says I to myself, there ain't nothing in it.[5]

Not receiving the fish hooks, Huckleberry Finn decided the prayer of petition was futile.

The question, "Does prayer influence God's will and effect changes in the world?" is a serious one because on reflection we recognize that an omniscient God does not need to be informed about our desires, nor does an all-good and all-loving God need to be encouraged to help us; nor is an omnipotent God hindered from coming to our aid without listening to our faltering analysis of our situations and our recommended solutions to them. Because of such questions the prayer of petition is the most debated component of the doctrine of prayer. Yet most Christians believe that petition is the heart and center of the life of prayer.

The second issue, seldom considered but especially germane to Protestants, is how to understand the link between human freedom and human sinfulness as it relates to prayer. Knowing what we want seems easy, but as sinners are we sufficiently wise and free to choose the subjects of our requests to God or are we too sinful even to know what we need? Unfortunately, most people exclude God's special providence from both the act of prayer and the selection of subjects for it. They suppose that while God's universal providence surrounds everything, our prayers belong to us. Most people assume we make our requests to God standing in human freedom outside God's particular providence with some independence rather than within and completely dependent on God's guiding love even in making our requests.

The question of the relationship between sin and free will is complicated. First it was possible not to sin. Then it was not possible not to sin, and finally it will not be possible to sin. Some theologians teach that Adam and Eve in the Garden of Eden had complete free will to choose to sin or to choose not to sin. When they chose to sin, the gift of free will was lost to all humans. Therefore, for people today, refraining from sin is impossible. In heaven, sin will not be possible. According to this teaching, freedom of choice existed in the past in the Garden of Eden but not in the present on earth (because of sinfulness) and not in the future in heaven (because of sinlessness). Certainly the Protestant Reformation emphasized the unfree will as is clear from the very title of Martin Luther's book, *Bondage of the Will*. Likewise, John Calvin insisted that the notion of free will gives human beings a foolish assurance about their own abilities. Calvin does not deny freedom of the will entirely because he accepts human responsibility and accountability. But he thinks that the focus on freedom of the will is always in danger of robbing God of his due honor (*Inst.* II.2.8). Christians, Calvin believed, should concentrate their attention on the grace of God and not on their freedom of the will. This conclusion does not resolve the issue, but tells Christians to concentrate on the glory of God. Understanding the miracle of prayer is unavoidably an exercise in doctrinal theology.

To address God rightly requires setting these two difficulties in a wider context. Prayer—a miracle of God's work in us and with us—includes an understanding of the role of human merit in our standing before God and a recognition of the mystery of God's responding.

Human Merit and Prayer

Prior to the Reformation two kinds of human merit were maintained: condign merit and congruent merit. Condign merit can be associated with Thomas Aquinas; congruent merit is associated with William of Occam. Protestants deny both understandings of merit and substitute a view that could be called "NO human merit." Protestants believe human beings stand before God not with condign or congruent merit, but with no merit. Christians can appear before God only as they are united to Christ. This Protestant view of "no merit" becomes clearer when condign and congruent merit are understood.

Congruent merit has four steps.

1. A person must make a small (and inadequate) effort toward salvation.
2. On the basis of that small effort God's sovereign grace is bestowed.
3. God's gracious bestowal enables a human response that God considers adequate.
4. Together, God's bestowal of grace and the human response to it leads to salvation.

Congruent merit has the advantage of avoiding the charge that God is arbitrary since human beings initiate the process of salvation. Salvation is also made dependent on the human desire for it rather than on divine love. Congruent merit can be illustrated by the process of buying a house. According to congruent merit, everything is conditional on a human effort. Thus, *if* (the condition) you want a nice house and *if* you make an appointment, then God will come by and show you what is available. *If* you select a house, then God will help you finance it. In this pattern, *if* you do not meet the conditions then you do not achieve the result.

Condign merit is a more widely accepted view. Salvation has three steps.

1. God's sovereign grace is bestowed on a person.
2. On the basis of God's gracious bestowal, an adequate human response is enabled.
3. God's initiating grace plus an acceptable human response produces salvation.

According to condign merit, God is sovereign over heaven and earth and initiates contact with human beings. The divine and primary initiative is called "operating" grace. The human and secondary response—also necessary—is called "co-operating" grace. Co-operating grace appears not to be part of God's direct providential care but of general and created human free will. This idea appears in the phrase "if you select" in the housing illustration. God is a landowner who has built all the quality houses in the subdivision called Earth. When and if God calls on you and volunteers to show a house to you, you may select one and God will help you finance it.

Although Reformed Christians are rightly uncomfortable with the word "merit," many of them harbor a view very much like condign merit because they cannot articulate the Protestant reversal of steps two and three. The "no merit" view of Reformed theology insists that (1) God's grace bestows (2) salvation on God's chosen ones, which then (3) results in human responses that are acceptable to God because of our union with Christ. The strength of the Reformed view is its offer of an account of salvation that depends on God's grace alone and not on human merit or decision. The Reformed view can be explained more fully this way:

1. God has created and redeemed the world.
2. God's creation and redemption includes you because inclusion is a gift of the Holy Spirit, called faith, which has two inseparable parts.
3. The first part of the gift of faith is justification or forgiveness, which means that in Jesus Christ God freely forgives sin once-for-all. The second part is called sanctification or holiness, which means that in Jesus Christ Christians are enabled to repent and more and more to lead saintly lives.

We have expanded on these themes in previous chapters. This no-merit view does not contain an even relatively separate human moment. That is, the human responsibility of "keeping the house clean and hospitable" is not conceived as outside God's direct providence. In fact, human responsibility is undertaken "with God's help." Reformed Christians believe God has custom-built a house for you and comes by to take you to it. Then God gives you the key and the deed with the admonition and expectation that you will keep your house clean and hospitable with God's help.

The conclusion of this discussion of human merit is that prayer is from beginning to end to be understood and, more importantly, practiced, within the sweep of God's wonderful grace in Jesus Christ. According to Calvin, Christ's atoning work includes his continual prayer for us. Our prayers are heard by God because they are united with the prayer of Christ, God's son (*Inst*. III.20.28–29). God does not answer our prayers because of any merit warranted by our faith, piety, or good works. God answers prayers because God loves us, and God wills that we trust that love by asking for our heart's desire as we grow into the mind of Christ (Phil. 2:5). With no merit of our own we can stand before God only in the merit of Jesus Christ to whom we are joined.

The Mystery of God's Responding

In Reformed theology, prayer is understood in terms of the Triune God. Prayer originates in faith, which is the gift of the Holy Spirit. Prayer is possible because the faithful are united with the Holy Son.

Prayer is certain because believers approach the Holy Father. The conviction that God is involved in our prayers led Calvin to define "prayer as the practice of predestination" (*Inst*. III.24.5). Calvin affirms that human asking cannot be separated from God's grace and denies the definition offered by a Roman Catholic theologian that "prayer . . . by definition cannot be a divine act since it is, above all, the act of man in the presence of God[.]"[6] Reformed theology insists that human being, created and redeemed, is not even relatively separated from God and therefore over against God in its freedom to pray. The human aspect of both faith and action for Reformed Christians is surrounded by the divine context and intent for human life. God's response to prayer is understood as a divine response to a divine initiative in the elect. The miraculous nature of petitionary prayer is captured in Calvin's statement, "But even though all these things must nonetheless come to pass in their time, without any thought or petition of ours, still we ought to desire and request them."[7] On the one hand, Calvin says all things must come to pass by God's will whether believers think about them or ask for them. On the other hand, Calvin insists that Christians ought not only to desire certain things but to request them. The intellectual difficulty is that one might desire and pray for what will inevitably come to pass as a way of submitting to God's ineluctable will even if it is logically possible that one's attitude of acceptance or rejection might itself be already determined. However, to request what will be forthcoming anyway seems both odd and futile. If prayer has no influence on the course of events, the only proper response would seem to be to accept one's circumstances rather than to request change. In short, for an individual to ask God to do what God will do anyway seems to be a form of accepting rather than a genuine request for one possibility to occur rather than another.

Calvin addresses this puzzling issue when he asks whether our prayers might get in the way of God's providence. That is, what is the propriety of informing God of what one believes God already knows or asking for help that God already desires to provide? Calvin's answer is that what God "has determined to give, of His own free will and even before He is asked, he promises to give all the same, in response to our prayers." According to Calvin, this conclusion is an "easy answer."[8]

For many of us this answer is not "easy." Still seeing how Calvin thinks about it is instructive. Calvin's comment on "work out your own salvation with fear and trembling: for it is God who works in you both to will and work,"[9] attacks the assurance that comes from blind confidence in one's own strength instead of depending completely on the grace of God. "It is God who works" means that believers can do nothing except through the grace of God alone. Calvin then distinguishes the two principal parts in any action—the will and the effective power—and says that *both are wholly ascribed to God*. God is not merely the author of the beginning of things and the end, but also of the middle. Calvin rejects the attempt to harmonize God's grace and human free will by conceiving free will as a human movement with peculiar and separate capacity. He recognizes that in this verse work is ascribed to divine being and human being in common. Some theologians derive human free will from the word "work" and find human merit in the process of salvation.

The proper understanding, according to Calvin, is that God brings to perfection those godly affections that God has inspired in us. Our duty is to request of God even those things that seem to come from our own hands. Both the good will and the good action should be credited to God's free mercy. Calvin admits that such a denial of human free will causes many people to indulge more freely in their vices, but he insists this abuse is not the fault of the doctrine of providence, which should bring the faithful to humble and careful prayer.[10]

The basic doctrine of prayer requires two affirmations that point to its miraculous reality. First, in divine wisdom and providence God anticipates our prayers. Second in divine love and providence God responds to our prayer. According to Calvin, Christians should not request more than God would freely bestow, but reminding God of what is promised to the faithful is not in vain. Moreover, Christians should refer to God all our needs, and even our wants as children familiarly address their father. We do this not to tell God what God does not know or argue with God about our needs, but to express the confidence that God will hear and respond to faithful petitions.[11]

Calvin refers to many kinds of asking and two kinds of obtaining. The faithful can ask without qualification for what God has promised, such as the perfecting of God's kingdom and the hallowing of his name, the forgiveness of sins and everything profitable to us. However

Christians are often mistaken when they imagine that God's kingdom must be furthered in a specific way, or that the hallowing of God's name requires a certain event. Therefore we are often deluded as to what tends to our own welfare. Christians can "ask for those things that are certainly promised with full confidence and without reserve, but it is not for us to prescribe the means, and if we do specify them, our prayer always has an unexpressed qualification included in it." For example, in asking for the removal of "a thorn in the flesh," Paul knew that "[i]f it had been to his advantage to be free of it, he would not have been refused."[12]

God's Prayer

Our prayer is God's prayer. Calvin makes this point clear in his Commentary on Jeremiah.

> [P]rayer is the fruit of repentance, for it proceeds from faith; and repentance is the gift of God. And further, we cannot call upon God rightly and sincerely except by the guidance and teaching of the Holy Spirit; for he it is who not only dictates our words but also creates groaning in our hearts. [It follows] that we do not pray through the impulse of our own flesh, but when the Holy Spirit directs our hearts, and in a manner prays in us.[13]

God's mercy is found in Jesus Christ on whom alone God's Spirit rests. Salvation depends on our union with Christ, who has changed God's throne from dreadful glory to marvelous grace because Christ's death is an everlasting intercession for us (*Inst.* III. 20.170). In other words, Christ's prayer for us is unceasing. Therefore when we pray we call on the name of God's son,[14] Jesus Christ our Lord, who always lives to make intercession for those who approach God through him (Heb. 7:15). The Christian doctrine of prayer can never lose sight of its divine basis and therefore never set the believer's will outside or over against the divine will that governs the world. God hears all the prayers of believers and God responds to them all, but not always in ways we desire or recognize. Nevertheless, God is in control of all our lives and all will be well. This teaching is summed up in familiar words from Romans 8:26–27:

Likewise, the Spirit helps us in our weakness; for we do not know how to pray as we ought, but that very Spirit intercedes with sighs too deep for words. And God, who searches the heart, knows what is the mind of the Spirit, because the Spirit intercedes for the saints according to the will of God.

13

The Use of Scripture

When I entered seminary the first scheduled activity was an examination in the content of the English Bible. I was not worried that I would be at the bottom of our class since we had among us some recent converts to the Christian faith and I figured, whatever other qualities they might possess, they could not know the Bible as well as I did. After all, I had many years of perfect Sunday School attendance, and our church had three worship services a week where scripture was expounded by a seminary-trained pastor.

I received the best grade on this test and was feeling rather smug about my biblical knowledge, until I overheard a visiting professor remark that in his country the poorest student would have made a better score than the best in our class. In addition, he suggested that preaching from the Bible in the United States would not be easy because the knowledge of its basic content was so very low among us and practically nonexistent among the congregations we would serve. I was offended at this offhand attack on my seminary class and my native land, and I also thought the comment was a terrible indictment of American Christianity. I wondered, could we really be so ignorant about the factual content of the scripture? In growing up I assumed everyone respected the Bible and that all intelligent adults had acquired a mature knowledge of scripture.

Obviously, before Christians can deal with the difficult and interesting question of interpretation of the Bible, they must know its content. Thus, toward the end of my first year as a pastor, I decided that finding out what my congregation actually knew about the Bible would be a good idea. I proposed to the officers that we take a few minutes in the Sunday worship service to give the congregation a simple true/false test, things like: True or False? "David lived after Moses," "Daniel was swallowed by a fiery whale," "Paul wrote the Book of Revelation," "Amos is concerned with justice." My senior officer said he thought this examination was a great idea, especially if I was thinking about looking for another pastorate in the near future! I took his point and dropped the idea of examinations. I learned from this situation that counting members and dollars was acceptable, but finding out what my congregation knew about the word of God was not. Our Sunday School was probably doing a good job among the children, but the Bible is not a children's book. Furthermore, scripture will have little effect on a congregation when decision-making adults are ignorant of it. I determined to try even harder to foster biblical literacy by teaching the adult Sunday School class and inaugurating a Wednesday night Bible study. After all, the content and interpretation of the Bible is the central focus of the ministry of Christ's church.

The Battle over the Bible

A great deal of ink has been spilled in the battle over the Bible because the camps are so far apart. To state the issue most simply: Is the Bible by its nature reliably perfect or perfectly reliable?

People who understand the Bible to be *reliably perfect* often employ the terms *infallible* and *inerrant*. Inerrancy means that the biblical text contains the direct and perfect word of God. Otherwise, so the argument goes, Christians could not trust the Bible to be true, and each Christian would be required to distinguish between true and false. Infallibility focuses not on a perfect text but on perfect teachings. The Bible contains no false teachings. Thus, to one group of Christians the words *inerrant* and *infallible* (together or singly) are absolutely essential to understanding scripture.

Christians who believe the Bible is *perfectly reliable* consider inerrancy and infallibility as nonessential. The terms are regarded as philosophical categories applied incorrectly to a historical document. This group points out that the famous slogan of the Reformation, "By

scripture alone," never actually stood alone. Protestants also confessed, "By Christ alone," and "By grace alone." In other words, three (!)
"alones" appear together. In this view, "scripture alone" does not stand
alone but is understood in the context of God's grace revealed in Jesus
Christ. Scripture need not be statically inerrant and infallible. Rather
the Bible is dynamically God's word for the company of the faithful.
The scripture is also a human word subject to all the conditions of
humanity—including making mistakes.

Arguments over the nature of scripture have divided American
Protestants for some time. Among the problems are the relation of
divinity and humanity and the relation of truth and authority.

At one end of the spectrum is the belief that "the Bible is God's
book" in the sense that God first dictates and then preserves the text
inerrantly and infallibly: the Bible has a divine nature. At the other
end of the spectrum is the conviction that the Bible is a human book
that contains only the words of men and women who experienced
God: the Bible has a human nature. Of course, many gradations
appear between these two positions.

The debate continues because some people assume that the establishment of biblical authority precedes the question of its truth. Their
reasoning goes as follows: The Bible is God's Word. God tells the
truth. Therefore, the Bible is true. In this way the truth of the Bible is
based on its identity as God's word. Since God is One (Deut. 6:4),
Christians are permitted to look for confirmation of the truth the
Bible contains, but its unity and authority are based on God's perfect
authorship. However, this view raises the horse-and-cart question.
Obviously, Christians want to put the horse before the cart, but which
is which? Is it necessary to commit to a theory of the inspiration of the
Bible before one has carefully considered every verse of every canon-
ical book? Put another way, for how long must individuals and groups
study each of the biblical books before they become competent to
insist upon a theory of inspiration that is to be applied to the Bible as
a whole? In fact, working out a doctrine of inspiration may take so
much energy that one does not have time to actually do interpretation.

Obviously God can and does use ignorant people to advance the
kingdom, but we normally assume that each person is obligated to
make a genuine effort to avoid ignorance, employing the best insights
available to us. The goal is the fullest possible understanding of scrip-

ture, but in the face of conflicting assurances of correctness, how is one to decide when this goal has been attained? To complicate the matter further, the Bible can profitably be approached in many ways: as literature, as history, as culture (i.e. , as the church's book and its role in a society), and devotionally. These approaches are all valuable, but for Christians the essential task is to hear and serve the Word of God. How, then, are we to understand the Bible as the Word of God? The imperative to hear the scripture as the Word of God leads to the suggestion that Christians focus on the *use* of the Bible rather than its *nature*.

Nature and Use

The centrality of the Bible means that if one has any theological views at all, they are likely to involve scripture. In fact, some people seem to have devoted more effort to developing a doctrine of scripture than to reading it. On some views the doctrine of scripture is the most fundamental of theological doctrines because it is the basis for all others. For many Christians the doctrine of scripture is already set and nonnegotiable. These persons are usually willing to consider a clearer presentation of their own view but resist all challenges to rethink it.

The role the Bible actually plays—as well as the role it ought to play—in the church is a complicated affair. This debate has been called a battle, and shots are still fired from all sides. Obviously, the proper defense of the right ground is crucial for the church, both present and future. While most mainline Christians are located somewhere between the inflexible fundamentalists on the hard right and the ever-flexible liberals on the loose left, a great deal of distance still must be covered before we can stand together comfortably as believers. On so central an issue the discussion must continue. However, consensus on the *nature* of scripture is extremely difficult to reach and perhaps even unnecessary. We suggest, therefore, that the church today could move forward by finding a consensus on the *use* of scripture. Today's church needs not a better *theory* of scripture but a better *practice* of scripture. Of course, the use of scripture is not expectation-free. Various kinds of people read the Bible with various purposes. Still, we need to remember doctrines are not themselves the content of faith, but guides to the faith. The Bible functions as our normative guide to lead us in faith. Christians may debate the Bible's nature but not its function. The church's immediate—indeed, urgent—task is to use the Bible.

The Living and Written Word

Before Christians consider the Bible as the Word of God, they need to affirm the Bible's own teaching that Christ is the eternal Word of God. "In the beginning [before the Bible] was the Word, and the Word was with God, and the Word was God." (John 1:1) While the ordinary means of our *knowing* the Triune God *follows* scripture, the *reality* of the Triune God *precedes* scripture. Put another way, the living Word, Jesus Christ, precedes the written word, the Bible.

The relation of these two forms of the Word of God leads to the question of whether Christian theology requires "a doctrine of scripture." The traditional answer, exemplified by the Westminster Confession (Article I), is a resounding, "Yes!" The assumption is that until you have worked out the nature of scripture, you can proceed no further with your theology because everything else depends on that doctrine. However, this position is not so self-evident as it might appear. For example, one can be well and properly married without having a *theory* of marriage. One may play an excellent game of chess without a doctrine of games. One may hit a baseball without being able to explain precisely how. In other words, the *use* of scripture and the *nature* of scripture, while closely related, are not finally identical.

John Calvin is cited by both sides in the current battle over the Bible, but the fact is that while Calvin's use of the Bible is massive, his remarks about its nature are few. Indeed, Calvin can serve as a model for the lifelong use of scripture with only minimal comment on the issues of its nature that vex us today. Good people have disagreed about the nature of scripture for a long time now, and the situation appears likely to continue. Most of us have a doctrine of scripture and consider those who differ from us to be wrong. However, small communities, like marriages, and large communities, like churches, can accommodate considerable differences of opinion when the will to do so is present. The modern issue of the nature of the Bible cannot be ignored, but it need not be the condition of our life together. On occasion the best way to find the right answer is to change the question.

Some important questions should be gently treated for the sake of fellowship. Two baseball fans can enjoy a game together without having to agree that Ty Cobb was greater than Babe Ruth; two music lovers can enjoy a symphony together without having to agree that Beethoven was greater than Mozart. Doubtless, the comfort level is higher where agreement is complete, but for a long time Americans have voted for either Republicans or Democrats and abiding by the results moved forward without insisting that everyone agree.

The most pressing issue today is not the nature of scripture but its use. Therefore, disagreements about the *nature* of scripture should be relegated to the background of our discussions so that Christians can concentrate on a common use of scripture that should strengthen our fellowship. Christians disagree about the exact nature of scripture, but they need not disagree about the necessary use of scripture.

All sides to this debate recognize and deplore ignorance of the Bible's content. The Bible has not fallen silent among us because its centrality is under attack.[1] Usually the Bible is thought of with respect, but modern life styles have made serious and continual Bible study an entirely optional activity that few choose to pursue. Use of the Bible in worship and education is also declining steadily. Preachers cannot expect enthusiastic understanding of sermons based on scripture. While the revelation of God is not to be equated with a book, revelation still comes to us only through the medium of that book. For Christians the study and exposition of scripture is not an optional activity. People who do not hear the voices of the biblical prophets and apostles will reflect only current cultural ideas and values.

The nature of scripture is important, and disagreements about this issue cause serious division. Nevertheless, a more serious problem among us is quite simply the ignorance of the Bible on all sides. Even if we could decide on a "right" doctrine of scripture, such a decision would not help much if people remain ignorant of the Bible's content. For that reason, Christians should make a more serious attempt to use the Bible. Too often Christians look in vain to find a serious use of scripture in the church. Many sermons make only casual references to scripture. Worship practices frequently ignore the Bible, and Christian education finds other lessons to teach and learn.

Quite apart from the complex question of its nature, the simple use of the Bible should be a sufficient challenge for most of us. The study of its content alone is a daunting and lifelong task. The study of its interpretation involves not only critical, literary, and historical research but also archaeological, philological, and comparative cultural studies. If Christians use the Bible with the seriousness it deserves, they will combine the desire for the best available human scholarship and the deepest passion to hear the divine word to God's people. As the Bible is read, studied, and preached, the astonishing good news of the gospel that Jesus Christ is Lord becomes sealed in people's hearts and minds. God has given this message in the Bible, which explains why using the Bible is more important than deciding on its nature.

The irenic statement in the Confession of 1967 found in the *Book of Confessions* of the Presbyterian Church (U.S.A.) contains much to commend it:

> The Bible is to be interpreted in the light of its witness to God's work of reconciliation in Christ. The Scriptures, given under the guidance of the Holy Spirit, are nevertheless the words of men, conditioned by the language, thought forms, and literary fashions of the places and times at which they were written.

This statement affirms both that God reveals God's will in scripture and that real human beings wrote the words that appear on the pages. "God has spoken his word in diverse cultural situations" requiring of us "literary and historical understanding" as we read "in dependence on the illumination of the Holy Spirit."[2] Moreover, since Christians confess the mystery of Jesus Christ as one person in two natures, accepting the mystery of the Bible as one book with two natures is possible as well.

14

The Blessings of Lamentation

The extent of evil in a world created by a good, loving, and acting God may be the single most difficult issue that Christians face. Each of us can come up with horror stories that pose this well-nigh unanswerable theological question: Why does a loving and all-powerful God allow evil, tragedy, and suffering? From my childhood, I remember a summer evening when a hit-and-run driver killed a little girl on my street. As a seminarian, I ministered over many months with a young father whose daughter was dying of leukemia. In faith he cried out in terrible anguish: "Where is God and why doesn't God heal my baby?" A young mother I knew died of cancer in her early thirties, leaving a husband and two little girls. And my own dear father died two days before my first son was born. My son's birth was announced to my extended family at my father's funeral. Why, I ask myself (and God), could he have not lived a few days more in order to have held his grandson?

Of the recent massacre in Rwanda, journalist Nancy Gibbs wrote that for hell on earth one only had to watch the rivers. As the rains come, the swollen rivers run red with the color of soil. But this time the rivers were swollen also with bodies: first men and boys float by, killed protecting their families. Then come the women and girls, cut down fleeing from their hiding places. Finally, the babies float by, thrown into the river to drown. Gibbs notes that in about half an hour, all the bodies drift by—just about the time needed to exterminate a community.[1]

Why does a loving God allow such terrible evil to take place? We have already treated this question in previous chapters. We move here to consider the place of lamentation in the face of suffering.

Psalm 30:5 reads, "Weeping may linger for the night, but joy comes with the morning." Let us not be too quick to jump to joy, however, for fear that we might miss the lessons to be learned from weeping: not a whimper and a sniffle—not the single, silent slide of a tear in the obscurity of propriety—but an abundant, sustained, and continual weeping, a weeping that lasts the night, a weeping that goes on and on. Numbers cannot count how much deep weeping comes in the silence of the night. Every pastor has some idea of the hidden depths of pain in his or her congregation when over 50 percent of marriages end in divorce, and one in three people will be a cancer patient. Some people are also aware of a secret weeping in our own hearts that, in spite of outward cheeriness and an apparent ability to function in public, endures year after year. And sometimes we watch fear and pain cripple the life of a colleague, a friend, or a neighbor, yet we are not invited in to share or to soothe. No one is a stranger to weeping, which is part of the parcel of life.

The Mystery of Suffering

An important distinction (as we indicated in chapter ten) can be made between a problem and a mystery. A problem is something you have some hope of solving or understanding. A great danger in speaking about suffering as a problem is that in our attempt to explain it we trivialize it, or even worse, turn it into an agenda for therapy. The fact is, a mystery cannot be understood but only endured. Philosophers and theologians have not found any entirely adequate answer to the problem of suffering, and they are not likely to do so. Suffering presents a deeper mystery than we can fathom. In fact, suffering is not an intellectual problem to be solved with rational thinking, but a real mystery to be approached with deep humility. Obviously, human sin lies deeply embedded in human suffering, whether an attempted genocide in Rwanda or a drunk driver hitting a child with his car. The fact is that we hurt one another. The mystery of natural disasters also confronts us weekly in the news and in our own communities; insurance companies call them 'acts of God.' Is that really what they are?

Can we just dump all the blame on God for all the evil and hurt in the world and think we have explained them? God could have created a world in which there was no cancer, or earthquakes, or genocides or wars or drunk drivers. Once we start on this line of thinking, however, our speculations can be both endless and groundless. Part of the moral problem lies with the fact that so much suffering is seemingly purposeless or pointless. And further, so much suffering is the result of evil in our midst. For Christian faith informed by scripture, however, suffering is faced in the context of relationship with God. On the one hand, we are compelled to name evil for what it is, and to combat it. On the other hand, reflection on the relationship between God and suffering forces the deepest question upon our minds.

1. God and Evil

This chapter is not about evil and the attempt to understand it, not an effort to write a theodicy. Our task now is more modest—namely, to reflect on suffering and to suggest a place for lamentation in our lives of faith. Yet saying something, however briefly, about evil is necessary, for much suffering is the result of evil. Evil is ultimately irrational in the sense that it contains no truth, and impersonal in the sense that evil stands counter to the personalizing love of God. Evil is a force for sin and death that stands opposite to the word of God. As the word of God is creative, evil is destructive. As God is love, evil is hatred of what is good. As God is personal, evil is monstrously impersonal, indeed, person-denying and person-destroying. People sometimes ask if one should believe in a personal devil. The concept of a personal devil is oxymoronic because the nature of the devil is to be impersonal, to be an 'it.' Evil exists as a negative reality, with no subsistence in itself. Its purpose is the destruction of that which is from God: creation, personhood, love, hope, joy, peace. Christian faith teaches that we can only see the Prince of Darkness for what it really is in the light shed by the word of God, in the light of the One who is the Light, the Prince of Peace.

Two things must be said about dealing with evil. First, before we can do anything about evil, we must acknowledge its power. Someone once suggested that the best lie the devil ever told was to suggest that the devil does not exist. Evil is a fact, and spiritual ignorance in this regard is not a moral option. Supposing that we can overcome evil without recognizing what we are dealing with is unacceptable theological naivete. Second, knowing what we are dealing with, evil must be combated. We are locked in a deadly spiritual battle. Evil will not win in the end; in fact the resurrection of our Lord already announces the demise of evil, but it exists still to wield its deadly venom and perverted attraction within the created order. Persons of faith are fighters for peace and justice, and advocates in all arenas of life for the dignity of persons and the rights of all creatures and the natural order. Attracted to the One who is the Light, Christians resist attraction to the occult, refusing to glamorize or sanitize evil as a form of entertainment. Faithful to baptism, Christians turn from the ways of sin and renounce evil and its power in the world, which defy God's righteousness and love.

2. God and Suffering

Psalm 30 raises some very difficult spiritual issues, the most challenging of which is that God is the cause of some of our suffering. The weeping that is the focus of Psalm 30 is for this specific reason deeply disturbing. The psalmist confesses that he once thought he had it made, once thought that he was secure: "As for me," he wrote, "I said in my prosperity, 'I shall never be moved.'" (v. 6) He had money, he had all he thought he needed for the good life. He was self-confident, relaxed in relying on his own achievements. No doubt he remained a pious man, but in truth he was his own center of attention. He was self-sufficient, unaware that his life depended upon God. In fact, he did not become aware that his life depended on the living God until a terrible thing happened: God hid his face, leading to a dreadful sickness. The psalmist faced the threat of imminent death, the reason for the lamentation.

God had hidden his face, and the psalmist now suffering from affliction unto death cries out to God in desperate supplication. The suffering is hard to bear. Perhaps, however, now prayer is really possible for the first time. His confession of sin and his appreciation of God's grace seem to coalesce in the one spiritual dynamic of new life and thanksgiving. The New Testament calls this dynamic *metanoia* or repentance, in this case a turn caused by God: "You have turned my mourning into dancing; you have taken off my sackcloth and clothed me with joy." (v. 11) The psalmist's experience is not of a vindictive, capricious God who visits affliction upon people for punishment, but of a God who in and through his suffering has brought him to a deeper understanding of himself and of God. The knowledge is of a God who has blessed him and renewed him and who is worthy of praise and thanks forever (v. 12). The image that endures is of a God who deals with us in our sin—and especially our tendency to self-worship.

The theological point to draw from Psalm 30 is that the psalmist only came to true knowledge of God when God apparently withdrew divine favor from him. Looking back on his old way of life, on his old attitudes, from the new perspective of someone who has traveled through the night of weeping and experienced the surprising and utterly gracious transformation made possible by God, he realized that God was the one who had disturbed his false peace, who had brought him near to death and caused his suffering and distress. The psalmist understood after the fact that God had pulled the plug on his smug self-sufficiency and destabilized his sense of security.

After the event, after the night of crying his eyes out, the psalmist realized that the withdrawal of divine favor and the experience of divine judgment were astonishing acts of God's love. The dark night of weeping was precisely the event that made possible the new morning of joy. The true joy of faith would not have been possible without a radical change in every aspect of the psalmist's life. In spite of the references to suffering and weeping, Psalm 30 is a psalm of thanksgiving, a looking back and saying, "Wow, look at what I was and at what God did to bring me from death to life." "O happy fall that brought us so great a redemption" was Augustine's theological maxim, in which he expressed what we find in Psalm 30.

This psalm brings us face to face with a profoundly awkward issue: the two hands of God, one acting in wrath, for God abhors our sin and our lukewarm religion, and one acting in love, to bring life from death. Accepting this twofold nature is very difficult for us. We want a cozy, comfortable God, a God who is nice, do we not? When we ask why bad things happen to good people, much modern theology ducks the hard issue by insisting that God is absent from the causes that affect us. On this view, God ends up on the sidelines, lamenting our suffering, surprised by the reality of evil, and ineffective to do any-thing about it. Understanding how an ineffectual God could be a basis for comfort is also difficult.

The Reformed tradition is made of sterner stuff! John Calvin addressed this difficult doctrine of God-caused suffering in his discus-sion of cross bearing in the *Institutes* (III.7.10). In a manner that par-allels Psalm 30, Calvin was concerned to show how God breaks human willfulness and our idolatrous sense of self-dependence. God does this, says Calvin, by afflicting a person with chastisement or med-icine or testing through which the sufferer learns to turn away from reliance on self and turn toward God. Led through many tribulations, says Calvin, Christians come to glory. Reading Calvin's writings, one wonders how much is theological autobiography. Calvin led a life of terrible suffering: death of a child, continuing illness, constant hurtful controversy. Yet Calvin himself accepted God-caused suffering. With regard to the death of his son he wrote, "The Lord has certainly inflicted a severe and bitter wound in the death of our infant son. But he is himself a Father, and knows best what is good for his children."[2]

The Transformation of Suffering

The Christian response to the mystery of suffering is not one of stoic resignation. Rather, faith invites a response that leads to the transformation of suffering. We will explore what this transformation involves in two ways. First, lamentation is an appropriate response to God, a response that may come in a variety of forms. The second is to explore briefly how suffering can be transformed to become a gift for ministry.

1. Lamentation as a Response to God

Once, when my wife was grating a carrot, she nicked the knuckle of her index finger, licked the wound, and carried on. A few days later, her finger was greatly swollen, her arm was inflamed, and she had pain under her arm. A telephone call to the doctor routed us quickly to the emergency room, where her finger was lanced and cleaned out, and on the way to being healed. The wound had closed, bacteria had been sealed in and had so infected the tiny nick that she was in danger of losing her finger. Similarly, emotional or spiritual wounds that are denied or left untreated fester and destroy us also from the inside out. Wounds of every sort need to be healed.

Truly, the vast mystery of evil is beyond our grasp, as we have said, but we can affirm that lamentation is a way of taking our wounds to God in trust that God wills to heal and bless us. Reflecting on the intellectual mysteries that evil and suffering raise is not enough. Being engaged in the battle with evil in private and public life is not enough. Taking our lead from biblical faith, we must also express the pain that we experience within the life of relationship with God. Buried within Psalm 30 is the psalmist's lament to God over his affliction.

> "O LORD my God, I cried to you for help." (v. 2)
> "To you, O LORD, I cried, and to the LORD I made supplication: 'What profit is there in my death, if I go down to the Pit? Will the dust praise you? Will it tell of your faithfulness? Hear, O LORD, and be gracious to me! O LORD, be my helper!" (vv. 8–10)

Lamentation does not explain suffering or even eliminate it, but crying out to God from the depth of our humanity is a part of its redemption.

One of the great theological crises in the Hebrew scriptures is the account of the fall of Jerusalem in 587 B.C. For two years the Babylonian army had surrounded Jerusalem with a siege that was ultimately so tight that neither food nor water could get in. Eventually the siege was successful and the leadership of the people was dragged off to exile in Babylonia. Behind them the Temple was burned to the ground, and Jerusalem and the major cities and fortifications were razed. King Zedekiah saw his sons slain before his eyes were put out, and he was brought to Babylon in fetters of bronze (2 Kings 25:7).

How did the exiles pray about this, when everything they had known, loved, and hoped for was so violently destroyed? The exiles were filled with bitter hatred against their captors and homesick for faraway Zion.[3] This experience was all the more profound, surely, because the prophets told them that the hand of God was to be found within their suffering. The fall of Jerusalem and the exile were events that contained important spiritual and theological meaning.

The Jews in exile prayed Psalm 137. The psalm names the yearning and hate that belong to every dislocated Jew.[4] In a general way this psalm could serve also all who know exile firsthand. Maybe it could also on occasion serve each of us when we spend a season of our lives weeping in the night.

> By the rivers of Babylon—
>   there we sat down and there we wept
>   when we remembered Zion.
> On the willows there
>   we hung up our harps.
> For there our captors
>   asked us for songs,
> and our tormentors asked for mirth, saying,
>   "Sing us one of the songs of Zion!"
>
> How could we sing the LORD's song
>   in a foreign land?
> If I forget you, O Jerusalem,
>   let my right hand wither!
> Let my tongue cling to the roof of my mouth,
>   if I do not remember you,
> if I do not set Jerusalem above my highest joy.
>
> Remember, O LORD, against the Edomites,
>   the day of Jerusalem's fall,
> how they said, "Tear it down! Tear it down!
>   Down to its foundations!"
> O daughter Babylon, you devastator!
>   Happy shall they be who pay you back
>   what you have done to us!
> Happy shall they be who take your little ones
>   and dash them against the rock!

No evidence survives that the psalm was a manifesto directing action against the babies of the Babylonians. No reason is given for suffering, nor to justify it in any way. The psalm is an expression of honest pain and bitterness given over to God and left in God's hands. Ultimately, vengeance belongs only to God (Rom. 12:19), and the giving over to God of our deepest negative human emotions is itself an act of astonishing liberation from the chains of hate that would otherwise bind us and suffocate the life out of us. Says Walter Brueggemann, "it is an act of profound faith to entrust one's most precious hatreds to God, knowing they will be taken seriously."[5]

A woman approached me after a talk I had given on lamentation. The crowded hall was slowly emptying and she tentatively approached the podium. "Do you mean what you said?" she asked. "Do you mean that I can really take my pain to God, my real pain, not covered up with nice words?" "Yes," I replied, "I believe that God wants us to be honest in our weeping, in our crying out to God in our pain." I asked her what lay behind her question. She told me that many years ago her young son, her only son, had died of leukemia. Her pastor and congregation had been wonderful in their support and love through that difficult time. But she felt still that something was unresolved about her son's death as far as her relationship with God was concerned. We talked briefly a while longer, and then someone else came forward to speak with me. But I saw her move off to a darkened corner by herself.

She was just within my earshot as I saw, out of the corner of my eye, that she balled her fists, raised them slightly upwards, and uttered a three-word prayer, one word repeated three times: I will not use the word in print, but I leave it to your imagination. Then she turned and walked away. I never saw her again. I regard her thrice-repeated word of anger and pain to be a prayer holy and acceptable to God who, in the death of his only begotten Son, knows what pain feels like. In God's grace maybe that day she experienced the turning from the night of weeping into the dawn of acceptance and a new day of joy.

There is no right or wrong way to pray our heart's desire to God. I heard the story somewhere of a pious Jewish father who had a mentally disabled son. The father rarely took the boy to the synagogue because he was unable to follow the service. One year, on the day of Yom Kippur (the Day of Atonement), the holiest day of the year, the father took his son to the morning service. The boy soon was caught up in the holy worship, and during the rabbi's long prayer he could contain himself no longer. But he did not know what to say or do. He remembered suddenly that he had put his old tin whistle in his pocket. As he pulled it out his stricken father clamped his hand over the boy's hand and told him to sit quietly. During the evening service, again the boy was with his father. Again the boy was caught up into the mystery of the holy worship, wanting to cry out in his need for God. Again, just at the point of the rabbi's prayer, the boy could contain himself no longer. He pulled out his whistle and gave it a loud blast. The rabbi stopped in his prayer for a moment, then continued. The prayer completed, he turned to his congregation and announced that the prayers of the people had risen to the Master of the Universe on the sound of the tin whistle! How important for us to learn to blow our tin whistles to God. That we blow them is the point, not whether we are in tune with everyone else.

2. Woundedness and Ministry

One November evening around six, I received a call from the wife of a student insisting that I come immediately to their seminary apartment. Her husband was lying on the floor coiled around the radiator, not moving. After reaching the apartment I was able to get him up and talking. The stress of forthcoming examinations had left him completely incapacitated. After a while the three of us held hands and prayed, then I drove them to the hospital. Later that evening as we sat together during his examination at the psychiatric clinic, he turned to me and expressed the conviction that his career as a seminarian and his hopes to be a minister were now over. Neither the seminary nor the church, he felt, would want someone who had a history of severe depression. I suggested that precisely because he was now dealing with his woundedness, entering into its mystery and pain for himself, and struggling with it in the light of his faith in God, ministry was now possible for him in a wholly new way.

One of the hardest lessons for people to learn is that their woundedness may be their biggest gift for ministry. Precisely because some of us have experienced weeping in the night are we able to sit alongside and minister to those who also weep. Henri Nouwen says in *The Wounded Healer* that "the great illusion of leadership is to think that man can be led out of the desert by someone who has never been there."[6] Learning the lessons of our own woundedness is a part of the spirituality of compassion that goes beyond the concern for techniques for ministry.

To be clear: the fact that something hurts is not the prelude to ministry filled with spiritual wisdom and insight. Rather we come to realize we must learn to speak the language of our own suffering in order to help another. Weeping in the night is not merely a flailing around in the dark; the weeping that occurs before God (and with God) enables us to move from death to life, from despair to joy, from help-lessness to ministry. Weeping may linger for the night—and for most if not all of us it will—but God uses our sadness for purposes that we can barely know or imagine while the weeping endures. Out of the struggle of living out and speaking forth our pain before God—lamentation—comes the rich treasury of gifted people who are then able to walk with others who suffer.

We see something of this theme in St. Paul, in 2 Corinthians 1:3–4: "Blessed be the God and Father of our Lord Jesus Christ, the Father of mercies and the God of all consolation, who consoles us in all our affliction, so that we may be able to console those who are in any affliction with the consolation with which we ourselves are consoled by God." By virtue of Paul's own suffering, and his consolation from God, he has a consolation to share with others in their suffering. If we have never suffered and received the consolation of God, we may have little to share with others in their time of need.

This lesson from St. Paul has been discovered in modern times by Alcoholics Anonymous, and various grief and cancer care organiza-tions. Frequently those people who have suffered, and walked through the dark valley of pain and loss, and had the courage and faith to shout it out to God, and who have found there the comfort and presence of God, are the individuals with special gifts for ministry. The journey with God into and through the mystery of our own suffering can become a gift of healing ministry for others.

In this chapter we have suggested various avenues of response for Christian people to the all-too-common human experience of weep-ing in the night. We proposed that suffering is a mystery to be entered into before God. Lamentation is an important part of living the mys-tery of suffering in the context of faith in God. Out of this aspect of the journey of faith comes the discovery of gifts for ministry to people who for a season also weep in the night.

15

The Certainty of Salvation

When I was in my early teens, one of my older friends often greeted me with the query, "Hey, kid, what do you know for sure?" I was not sure I knew anything for absolutely certain, but at least I was sure that I did not want an argument about the difference between appearance and reality or between knowledge and opinion. So I always answered, "Nothing much."

Some years later in an introductory philosophy course I ran across the same question put more seriously. The philosophers wondered, "Can anything be known for certain?"[1] Until then I had assumed that at least some adults knew the answers but could not share them with those who had not prepared themselves by careful study. Now I realized how difficult the question was. Still, I thought, surely everything is not ambiguous. The truth must exist, and when I found it I would be certain of it. But instead, what seems to have happened is that as I age I just have more sophisticated doubts.

A few Christmases ago I received some books by a well-known Christian writer. After reading these books I concluded that I would be happy to be as certain about anything as this author was about everything! I was amazed that the writer could have such strong opinions about so dizzying a range of intellectual disciplines. His books were designed not to discuss the complicated issues but to deliver definitive answers to them. On the few topics where I had spent considerable time and effort I felt entitled to disagree with his conclusions. This disagreement made me uneasy about other places where I strongly suspected he was wrong. Nevertheless, he was much impressed with his own performance, and if he made any mistakes no shadow of a doubt fell across his pages.

Just as with this writer, for many people being passionately sincere seems to be more persuasive than actually being right. Apparently if you are sincere enough about a topic, you are probably right about it, too. On the other hand, many people associate all certainty with arrogance. In being humble we can try to avoid being dogmatic and often end up just being skeptical.

Most of us have serious doubts all our lives: Does she (or he) really love me? Do I deserve a raise? Will I succeed? Every assertion we make can be countered by the question, "Are you sure?" Thus, the door that leads to the room for doubt is never locked. At the same time, on some subjects ambiguity makes us uncomfortable and we seek assurance or reassurance. Everyone who raises a question about fact—and that includes all of us at least some of the time—is expressing some kind of doubt. Doubt may be defined as the conviction that the claim to truth is obscure and the evidence advanced to demonstrate it is inadequate. The overcoming of doubt points us in the direction toward certainty, but our arrival there is not assured. The process of assertion and denial, question and answer, counterquestion and counteranswer seems woven into the fabric of the human condition and not to be separated. One can assume among human beings that the certainty of doubt is self-evident. Nothing, we say sardonically, is certain except death and taxes.

Nevertheless, Christians at least would like to be assured of God's pardon. That is, we desire to be completely forgiven for our sins and to know that God loves us and will save us. At the same time, many people harbor serious doubts about the certainty of their personal salvation. Some Christians assume that the assurance of pardon is really contingent—not actual but only possible. Conditional pardon means that *if* certain conditions are fulfilled, only *then* will certain results occur. For example, *if* she believes ABC or does XYZ *then* she will be saved, otherwise not. Obviously, if forgiveness is conditional, salvation is never assured and doubt is as certain as faith. The certainty of doubt, then, appears to lead to the doubt of certainty.

This chapter addresses not the general certainty of doubt but the general doubt of certainty concerning salvation, insisting that individual

Christians cannot doubt that their salvation is certainly accomplished and graciously bestowed in Jesus Christ. This definition does not describe how Christians actually think, since persons are always capable of doubting every affirmation. The definition maintains that Christians ought to accept the assurance of their pardon as the real consequence of God's grace. That is, Christians should doubt their doubts about salvation and trust in the mighty love of God revealed and extended in Jesus Christ.

Protestant Certainty and Catholic Doubt

An almost forgotten mark of the Protestant Reformation is the conviction that salvation is not conditional but certain! Early Protestants believed one's salvation was known to the believer. John Calvin, for example, insisted that to doubt the certainty of our salvation was sinful. According to Calvin we do not understand the goodness of God unless we gather the fruits of full assurance (*Inst.* III.2.16). Again, Calvin writes that scripture always attributes to faith a "feeling of full assurance." "[F]aith is not content with a doubtful and changeable opinion . . . but requires full and fixed certainty. . . ." (*Inst.* III.2.15) Commenting on Romans 8 Calvin says, "The first and chief consolation of the godly in adversity is to be persuaded *for certain* of the fatherly kindness of God." This kindness includes the certainty of salvation, which is a knowledge that comes "not, as some sophists falsely state, by special revelation, but by *a perception common to all the godly.*" If, Calvin claims, the doctrine of election were buried in the secret counsel of God and believers' salvation *not* known to them, election "would have been a doctrine not only lacking in warmth, but completely lifeless." As a matter of fact even a lot of people who admire Calvin think predestination is a doctrine so hidden in the secret counsel of God that nobody can know for certain that they are saved. Against that mistaken view Calvin insists, "our faith is nothing, unless we are persuaded for certain that Christ is ours, and that the Father is propitious to us in Him. There is, therefore, no more pernicious or destructive conception than the scholastic dogma of the uncertainty of salvation."[2]

In these quotations Calvin makes three important points. First, salvation is certain. Second, salvation can be certainly known to the elect;

the elect have full assurance of pardon. Third, election is a lively and comforting doctrine. These three assertions about certainty involve the doctrine of predestination since the elect are the ones who have assurance of their salvation. The identification of the elect is both complicated and crucial. However, on the topic of certainty, Reformed theology answers the question, "What do you know *for sure*?" with, "I know I am surely saved by my Lord, Jesus Christ!" Accordingly, whatever items might be appropriately doubted, one's salvation is not among them.

The Roman Catholic Church takes a different stance. In his *Summa Theologica* Thomas Aquinas considers the question of "certitude" by asking whether we can know we have grace. He answers that we can know by a direct revelation of God, but not otherwise.[3] According to Thomas (and Roman Catholic theology), the certainty of one's own salvation can be known by special revelation, but such certainty is not the normal condition of believers.

This issue is seen in the debate between Martin Luther and Desiderius Erasmus, a humanist scholar and theologian. In the Protestant Reformation, Martin Luther and John Calvin claimed a personal assurance of being forgiven that Erasmus and the Roman Catholics denied. The Council of Trent, which formulated the Catholic response to the Protestant Reformation, insists, "No one [can] state with absolute certainty that he is among the number of the predestined[.] For except by special revelation, it cannot be known whom God has chosen to Himself."[4] Today, sadly, the doubt of certainty probably applies to both Catholics and Protestants. However, Luther thought that for Roman Catholicism the scriptures were considered obscure so that people were supposed to trust the apostolic see of Rome. According to Luther, the denial of the certainty of salvation was terrible. The truth is "through the enlightening of the Holy Ghost, the special gift of God, one enjoys complete certainty in judging of and deciding between the doctrines and opinions of all men as they affect one's self and one's own personal salvation."[5] Speaking before an assembly at Worms (1521), Luther declared the standard of true knowledge to be "the testimony of Scripture and manifest reasoning."[6] Interestingly, in this formulation, scripture does not stand alone, which indicates that the Protestant appeal to scripture is more complicated than some people think. Still, however profound the issues might be, the Protestants were claiming the superiority of scriptural authority over ecclesiastical authority. As we have seen, John Calvin sided with Luther in refusing to doubt the certainty of salvation.

Luther's learned opponent, Erasmus of Rotterdam, disagreed. Erasmus thought nothing could be known for sure, and to this cool anti-intellectualism he added a warm, devout, and undogmatic Christian piety, a religion of moral decency that included a calm and skeptical resignation to ecclesiastical authority. When Luther asserted he was teaching the biblical truth, Erasmus responded, "How can we know for sure?" According to Erasmus, since nobody can be certain, accepting the tradition of the church as it has understood the Bible through the centuries is more reasonable than to assume that scripture and tradition are in conflict as Protestants insist. In his 1503 book, *Enchiridion* (or *Handbook of the Christian Soldier*), Erasmus put forward his vision of an inward religion based on the ethical implications of the wisdom revealed in the teachings of Jesus Christ. This inwardness leads to an individualism that fosters apprehension rather than certainty about salvation. The Council of Trent concludes that a person who boasts of the "certainty of the remission of his sins [preaches] with untiring fury against the Catholic Church. . . . For as no pious person ought to doubt the mercy of God, the merit of Christ and the virtue and efficacy of the sacraments, so each one, when he considers himself and his own weakness and indisposition, may have fear and apprehension concerning his own grace, since no one can know with the certainty of faith, which cannot be subject to error, that he has obtained the grace of God."[7] Accordingly, one may not doubt the mercy of God, the merit of Christ, and the efficacy of the sacraments, but one must deny the certainty of faith.

The Basis of Certainty

For centuries a debate has persisted between people who think some things can be certainly known and people who think probable opinion is all we have to guide our lives. In a recent book, Allan Bloom claims, "There is one thing a professor can be absolutely certain of: almost every student entering the university believes, or says he believes, that truth is relative." Nothing is certain because everything is relative. That is, some things may be truer than other things, but only in relation. Nothing is absolute or unconditional truth. According to Bloom, for today's students, the "relativity of truth is not a theoretical insight but a moral postulate, the condition of a free society. . . . They believe that relativism is necessary to openness, which is "the only plausible stance in the face of various claims to truth. . . ."[8] Presumably, many people consider skepticism with regard to all claims for truth and certainty as normal.

Some doubts are good for us. When something is not clear or obvious, being doubtful is beneficial. However, most of us learn that what once seemed clear turns out later to be clearly wrong. Continual questioning often leads to real progress. Every possible affirmation can be challenged by the question, "Are you sure?" This question ordinarily asks only for degrees of certainty, and the answer, "Sure enough," is usually sufficient. Still, for some crucial questions we long for absolute certainty. For example, we want to believe that our work is meaningful, our friends true, our health real. Most of all, Christians yearn to know salvation is certain.

Many Protestants today may be surprised, therefore, to learn the Reformers taught that one's salvation is certain and can be certainly known. Perhaps, they think, one could accept the certainty of salvation as foreordained or foreknown by God, but, since human beings are so far from the divine being, maintaining personal certainty of salvation seems arrogant. To the contrary, however, Martin Luther insisted "that God has taken my salvation out of the control of my own will, and put it under the control of His, and promised to save me, not according to my working or running, but according to His own grace and mercy. *I have the comfortable certainty* that He is faithful and will not lie to me, and that He is also great and powerful, so that no devils or opposition can break Him or pluck me from Him."[9] Notice that our certainty of salvation is located in God and not in ourselves.

In ourselves we live in turmoil. Calvin recognized that Christians experience both belief and disbelief. The two halves of the statement, "I believe and yet have unbelief," appear to contradict each other, but all of us experience both.[10] Calvin continues, "Therefore the godly heart feels in itself a division because it is partly imbued with sweetness from its recognition of the divine goodness, partly grieves in bitterness from an awareness of its calamity; partly rests upon the promise of the gospel, partly trembles at the evidence of its own iniquity, partly rejoices at the expectation of life, partly shudders at death." (*Inst.* III.2.18) The conflict between certainty and doubt "is what every one of the faithful experiences in himself daily, for according to the carnal sense he thinks himself cast off and forsaken by God while yet he apprehends by faith the grace of God."[11]

Nevertheless, Calvin insists, we should "stand before God in the sure confidence of divine benevolence and salvation [because a believer is] convinced by a firm conviction that God is a kindly and well-disposed father towards him, promises himself all things on the basis of his generosity; who, relying upon the promises of divine benevolence toward him, lays hold on an *undoubted* expectation of salvation." (*Inst.* III.2.15,16; emphasis added) This lack of doubt is possible because we are "sealed with the Holy Spirit," meaning that the assurance which believers have of their own salvation comes from the Holy Spirit "who makes their consciences more certain and removes all doubt." "Let us remember," Calvin writes, "that the certainty of faith is knowledge, but it is acquired by the teaching of the Holy Spirit, not by the acuteness of our own intellect."[12]

Two major modern modes of thought hinder accepting the Reformation teaching about the certainty of salvation. First, some Christians locate certainty in an objective relation with the Bible. The Bible is regarded as the way to God rather than the witness to God. This view locates truth and therefore certainty in the Bible understood as objective truth from which fundamental doctrines can be logically deduced. A more adequate interpretation holds that the Bible is the written Word of God that testifies to the living Word of God, Jesus Christ.

The second hindrance, currently more popular but equally erroneous, is the rampant individualism which means for many modern people that religion, including Christianity, is essentially a matter of personal experience, of feeling, of individual and private "spirituality." This misunderstanding is compounded by the modern assumption of a human self separate from God. The self is often defined, even by Christians, in terms that include God's creation of persons but exclude

God's redemption of persons except as a conditional offer. On this view creation is an obvious and necessary fact, but salvation becomes just a possibility offered by God to be realized by us. Obviously worshiping a book is dangerous, as is worshiping the self.

Christian thinking should begin as twentieth-century theologian Emil Brunner reminds us, with "inquiry on the part of believers into the source, the foundation, and the norm of their faith—which can be no other than the Word of God become flesh in Jesus Christ."[13] Brunner here describes the affirmation of our "union with Christ." Obviously believers are not identical with Jesus. We remain the "old" Adam and Eve, but we also know "if anyone is in Christ, there is a new creation: everything old has passed away; see, everything has become new!" (2 Cor. 5:17) Again, "you have died, and your life is hidden with Christ in God. When Christ who is your life is revealed, then you also will be revealed with him in glory." (Col. 3:3–4)

Because of life and faith in Christ, Christians affirm both our certain origin in God's creation and our certain salvation in God's redemption. Although this certainty does not answer all questions or resolve all difficulties, in denying human merits it fosters the deepest humility before God's grace revealed in Jesus Christ and applied to us by the power of the Holy Spirit. The certainty of salvation is based not on the contented heart curved in on itself but the grateful arms thrown open to God's mighty love in Jesus Christ. The certainty of salvation is grounded in our Lord and what he has done for us. Assurance comes through the gift of faith—the principal work of the Holy Spirit—and is received with humility, gratitude, and thanksgiving.

In this certainty the human mind rises above its natural capacity and becomes persuaded of what it cannot grasp. Paul expresses this notion when he writes that Christians know the love of Christ which surpasses knowledge (Eph. 3:18–19). This knowledge consists more in assurance than in comprehension. Calvin thought that God who has promised to be faithful intends to uproot doubts from our hearts so that faith may have "full and fixed certainty." (*Inst.* III.2.14–15)

The fearless certainty of salvation can be summarized in the Trinitarian words of the first question and answer of the Heidelberg Confession:

Q: What is your only comfort, in life and in death?
A: That I belong—body and soul, in life and in death—not to
     myself but to my faithful savior, *Jesus Christ*, who at the cost
     of his own blood has fully paid for all my sins and has com-
     pletely freed me from the dominion of the devil; that he pro-
     tects me so well that without the will of *my Father* in heaven
     not a hair can fall from my head; indeed, *that everything must
     fit his purpose for my salvation.* Therefore, by *his Holy Spirit*, he
     also *assures me of eternal life*, and makes me wholeheartedly
     willing and ready from now on to live for him. (Emphasis
     added)

Belonging—body and soul, in life and death—to our faithful savior
Jesus Christ is the basis of Christian certainty.

16

The Reality of Hope

Nicole was a lovely baby, under a year old—full of life, an icon of hope for her parents—when suddenly illness struck. I first met Nicole when her belly had already grown huge with the tumor that was soon to kill her. I had taken a shop-floor summer job during the university vacation, and I worked alongside Nicole's father, who had forsaken college in order to provide for his family. We quickly became friends, and slowly he began to share the story of his baby's cancer and the agonizingly unsuccessful medical treatments. Near the end of that summer he invited me for dinner in their small apartment. I saw Nicole for the first time. Her dying was drawn out for a few more months, painful for her and overwhelmingly devastating for her very young parents. I recall Nicole's funeral as profoundly sad. I confess, too, to an anxiety. As a first-year theological student, what should I say to my new friends whose hope for healing for their daughter was now lying like a shipwreck all around them?

On the outskirts of San Salvador lies the Catholic parish of Calle Real, astonishingly misnamed the "royal road," for the location is a place of truly amazing dereliction and neglect. In 1993, just after the end of the twelve-year civil war, acrid smoke from the cooking fires filled the air, the unrepaired damage of war overwhelmed the eyes, ragged children played soccer on scrub land, and yapping mongrel dogs hoping for food followed every movement. On first glance it is hell. The Catholic priest in Calle Real was an American, and we attended Sunday morning mass, a festival of life celebrating the meager harvest. In the midst of grinding poverty the people brought gifts to lay before God. They sang and danced and laughed. The patron saint of the parish was paraded around the church, with banners and streamers in abundance. Afterwards, outside, women of the church prepared lunch over huge open fires. I wrote in my journal: "The image which has emerged for me at Calle Real is 'fruit of the word.' This is hope, God is here, life in the midst of death."

What can Christian faith say to Nicole's grieving parents that might give them hope in the face of her tragic death? What is the nature of the hope that empowers the people of Calle Real, to dance for joy in praise of God in the face of poverty and the ravages of war? An account of the hope of the gospel must meet the challenge of these questions or be rendered worthless. Even worse, the hope of the gospel becomes an offense in the face of the terrible suffering it seeks to address. The challenge of hope compels us to speak of life in the face of death. Hope affirms that life and not death has the last word. How is this possible?

Questions Put to Hope

Keeping in mind Nicole, her parents, and the people of Calle Real, three interrelated issues need to be addressed:

1. Hope must deal with death.
2. Hope must address embedded sin and forgiveness.
3. As Jesus Christ is Lord over all of life, a theology of hope must anticipate the transformation of the world.

1. Hope Must Deal with Death

While the denial of death may well be a public feature of our society, death nevertheless is both all around us and at work within us (2 Cor. 4:12). We may, with the philosophers, muse on the value of death, yet its terrible finality presses upon us. A theology of hope is compelled to address the issue of what happens when we die. Such a theology must tell us how we can have hope when we know we will die. Does death not finally make a mockery of Christian hope?

2. Hope Must Address Embedded Sin and Forgiveness

Whatever else sin is, it is a power for destruction whose effect transcends the moment. The curse of sin lies not only in its momentary consequence, in which we oppose God, but also in its capacity to carry on with its evil into the future. A timely example will illustrate. My mother's parents were Irish Catholic. I recall as a youngster in Edinburgh how when my mother's family would be in town we would all gather around the coal fire, and I would be fascinated by the Irish lore that would be told long into the evening. Only later in life did I realize that in and through the stories the dangerous memory of bitterness and anger against the English was being nurtured and passed on from generation to generation. My Scottish Presbyterian father used to say that the curse of the Irish was that they would not forget. I must add that they, both Protestant and Catholic, would also not forgive, and that sin endured for evil in the collective memories on both sides. So the question is, what is the meaning of Christian hope in the context of embedded sin?

3. Hope Must Anticipate the Transformation of the World

A hope promised by the gospel that did not seek to bear witness to the reign of God in the midst of economic and political experience would be no hope at all. A theology of "sweet by and by when you die" is no comfort for the millions of people who live amid violence, disaster, poverty, ill health, poor education, malnutrition, and so on. A theology of hope must be a practical theology that not only describes the basis for hope but also provokes transformations in history.

Christians are charged to give an account for the hope that is the gift of the gospel (1 Peter 3:15). In meeting this theological responsibility we must address not only the obvious concerns around death and sin, but also the profoundly biblical concerns for justice and peace. These concerns are not merely academic, fit only for the theology classroom. For not just the cogency of Christian hope is at stake here, but also the possibility of life lived with liveliness and the power to transform the vicious cycles of death, violence, and sin into processes that make for life.

The Reality of Hope

For Christians, to speak of hope is to speak of Jesus Christ. Perhaps that point may be made most strongly by paraphrasing the familiar introduction to John's Gospel: In the beginning was the hope, and the hope was with God, and the hope was God. The hope was in the beginning with God, and the hope became flesh and dwelt among us. In this context, we can see clearly that while the Christian's hope has to do with the Christian hoping, it has more—much more—to do with who God is and what God does toward us. In thinking about hope we do not just think about hoping as a psychological state, but we think about Jesus Christ who is our hope, even whether we feel hopeful or not.

Jesus is the subject matter of the Christian's hope. Although hope has value as a personal experience—for hope is a gracious human experience in the face of suffering and death, a blessed experience, and a miracle—hope for the Christian is not derived from reflection upon our own experiences, at least not first of all, because Jesus is the hope of the gospel. Christian hope is not a self-reflective, circular process whose point is "I am hopeful because I have hope." Hope stemming from such a process becomes our possession. The enemy of hope would then be despair. Pastorally, such an understanding of hope would mean casting Nicole's parents back upon themselves to find hope within, amazingly cruel in the face of so devastating a loss.

The identifying feature of evangelical theology is its assumption that we are addressed from outside of ourselves by a word that reveals God to us on God's terms and that constrains our response accordingly. In evangelical theology we try to think and live from a center in God, because God is not mute and because the relationship between God and ourselves is restored in and through Jesus Christ. Hope can then be understood in a distinct—that is, a Christian—way. In such a view, hope is not a possessive affection or even an act of human will, but an act of God in which we have faith and trust. We have to think of hope as having a basis in God, in which we participate by grace through faith. We dare to believe that for the people of Calle Real the surety of God's deliverance, and not their reliance on their own affective dispositions of faith, enables them to dance and sing in the *barrio*.

We turn now to discuss the three issues raised above.

1. Death and Hope

In the New Testament hope is based on the resurrection of Jesus. "By his great mercy (God) has given us a new birth into a living hope through the resurrection of Jesus Christ from the dead." (1 Peter 1:3) "God raised the Lord and will also raise us by his power." (1 Cor. 6:14) In the Gospel of John at 14:19 Jesus says, "because I live, you also will live." According to Acts 23:6, Paul is on trial concerning hope and the resurrection of the dead. Putting it now negatively, "If Christ has not been raised . . . faith has been in vain." (1 Cor. 15:14) Further, as St. Paul said, "If for this life only we have hoped in Christ, we are of all people most to be pitied." (1 Cor. 15:19)

Is Jesus only a moral teacher, a sage who can give us insight into and meaning for life, but who is powerless to give eternal life? If we hold that belief, Paul says, we have missed the point. The early Christians believed that the resurrection was not only a sign that Jesus was alive, but also a guarantee that they would live also beyond death. First, then: hope trusts that what happened to Jesus will happen to Nicole.

Note that the funeral service is not called the "Service of Christian Hope," as if now, at the last, everything is to be cast back upon ourselves, our faith, our hopes, and our theories of eternal life. Rather, the funeral service is called the "Witness to the Resurrection," which is a profoundly instructive title. At this point, everything is cast back upon Jesus Christ—into whose future we trust ourselves—and we pray to God for the faith to rest in that trust. Hope does not point back to itself; rather, hope points away from itself to the risen, present Christ. In the Commendation at the end of the funeral service we read:

> You only are immortal, the creator and maker of all.
> We are mortal, formed of the earth,
> And to earth shall we return.
> This you ordained when you created us, saying,
> "You are dust,
> and to dust you shall return."

> All of us go down to the dust;
> yet even at the grave we make our song:
> Alleluia, alleluia, alleluia.[1]

In the tradition of John Calvin, we affirm that faith believes that eternal life has been given to us in Jesus Christ. Hope anticipates that at some time this eternal life will be revealed. What faith believes, hope expects. Faith is the foundation, and hope nourishes and sustains that faith. Hope has the same goal as faith, namely, a confidence in the benevolence of God toward us. This confidence is founded upon the promise given in Christ, revealed to our minds through scripture, and sealed upon our hearts by the Holy Spirit.

Where was God when Nicole died and when her parents struggled so hard to deal with their dashed hope for a medical miracle that would have kept their baby alive? Perhaps the harshest but most honest form of atheism lies not with the denial of God's existence but with the assumption that God is only a spectator to the tragedies of life. So what if God has promised resurrection of the dead if God just sits on the sideline cheering us on, letting us fend for ourselves in the midst of seemingly pointless death? Is the God of hope powerless—or even worse, callous and indifferent—in the face of present sufferings?

If the resurrection of Jesus is the basis for what we believe about and expect from God, the raising of Jesus itself cannot be understood apart from the events that occurred three days before in the Christian story, on the day Christians call "Good Friday." What makes this Friday good? Christian tradition has sometimes noted that Good Friday is the day of the Father, Easter the day of the Son, and Pentecost the day of the Spirit. Is this not backwards, for surely Good Friday is the day of the Son, the day of the death of Jesus, and Easter the day of the Father, when Jesus was raised by the power of God? We can say that Good Friday is the day of the Father because the cross casts a dark shadow over God, affecting God and, as it were, giving a new meaning to God's divinity. The cross as a Jesus event is thereby also a God event. God did not deal with Jesus by acting as an untouched, outside agent. The cross was not only an event that ended a man's life; it was also a God event that makes this Friday good.

God in Christ has entered into the darkness of death and brought life to light. In the cross God has chosen to make God's home with

Nicole in her dying and her parents in their bereavement, and with the people of Calle Real in their poverty and abandonment in war-torn El Salvador. God is not far off, a disinterested cosmic spectator to the deadly dramas of our human history, but an active participant who, in the continuing presence of Christ through the Holy Spirit, with compassion knows the human predicament from the inside. A cross is always present in the heart of God. God, said the English philosopher Alfred North Whitehead, is the fellow sufferer who understands.

Elie Wiesel, a survivor of Auschwitz and Buchenwald, describes in his book *Night* the execution of two men and a boy by the SS. His reflection takes us into the heart of the compassion of God. As the three necks were placed into the nooses, Wiesel recalls that the adults called out, "Long live liberty!" The boy was silent. Someone behind him then asked out loud, "Where is God?" The adults died quickly, but the boy, being so light, dangled a while longer. Wiesel reports that a second time he heard the person behind him ask out loud, "Where is God now?" And then he tells us he heard within himself an answer in reply that says that God is there, hanging on the gallows.[2]

The God event of Good Friday tells us that God is with us in the deadly situations of life. God is always Emmanuel, God with us, in Jesus Christ. God has entered into our life unto death in order to bring life and hope to light. Pastorally, the first word of hope for the parents of Nicole is that God is with you, and God knows your grief because the Father knows the grief of the death of his beloved Son.

2. Hope for Sinners

The hope of the gospel is not only a future in God for those who suffer, the dying, and the abandoned, but also a future in God for sinners. Every pastor recognizes the extent to which so many people lack confidence in their salvation, not sure that their sin is really forgiven. As we showed in chapter 6, the finality of forgiveness is a complex issue. We argued that God's gift is to give the assurance of salvation. Another way to look at the finality of forgiveness, however, is to think of it also as a basis for hope. The hope of the gospel is not only in Christ's at-one-ment with us in our suffering unto death, but also in Christ's atonement whereby we are forgiven by God and clothed with the righteousness of Jesus Christ. Romans 4:25 was a favorite text of both John Calvin and John Knox: Jesus Christ our Lord "was handed over to death for our trespasses and was raised for our justification." Atonement for sin and the bestowal of a positive righteousness belong here entirely to the work of Christ, culminating in the resurrection. The declaration of forgiveness through Jesus Christ is absolutely central to the proper understanding of the gospel and Christian hope. For this reason, the confession of sin and the declaration of forgiveness have such important places in Christian worship. In Christ, and through the Holy Spirit, God has reached into the lostness of our humanity to hold us firmly by the hand and lead us into communion with God for eternity.

An image I heard from my former teacher in Edinburgh, Tom Torrance, explains something of our understanding of hope. He tells of remembering quite vividly teaching his little daughter to walk. Many decades later, he could still feel the touch of her hand in his hand. And when she would stumble his hand held her firm. Torrance used this image to speak of our new life in God through Jesus Christ. Stumbling around, on the verge of toppling into the vast abyss of sin unto eternal death, Christ grasped us: "even there your hand shall lead me, and your right hand shall hold me fast," said the Psalmist (139:10). When we in faith, as a gift of grace, reach to hold the hand of God, we discover that we are already held securely, for God's hand is upon us (Ps. 139:5). Our hope for salvation does not lie in the fact that we hold on to God's hand, as if our decision and act were part of the economy of hope. Rather, our hope for salvation lies in the fact that God's hand in the humanity of Jesus Christ has already reached out for and found and holds fast to our hand. The radical consequence of sin forgiven and the bestowal of a positive righteousness is that we place no trust in our own goodness, piety, or good works. We place our hope entirely in the grace of Christ alone. As sung in Augustus Toplady's hymn "Rock of Ages,"

> nothing in my hands I bring;
> only to thy cross I cling.

In the hope of the gospel we expect a future beyond death on the basis of Christ's cross and resurrection. We have hope also for our sinful pasts, and our coming sinful futures of disobedience and faithlessness, on the basis of Christ's atonement and our restoration into a new relationship with God in him. This hope is not that God someday will break the vicious cycles of death, destruction, and violence that characterize our living, or that we will suddenly receive the message and begin to live ethically. The faith is that God in Jesus Christ already has entered into the vicious cycles, turned them from death to life, and restored us to a new humanity that we are called day by day to live out in faith, love, and gratitude.

3. The Reign of God and the Transformation of the World

Turning now to the third question raised in the previous section, we will discuss the significance of the reign of God for the politics of hope. In the midst of Nazi Germany, Dietrich Bonhoeffer somewhere once reminded the church that "only those who cry out for the Jews may sing Gregorian chants." Perhaps also only those who cry out for the people of Calle Real, and all who suffer unjustly, may sing Gregorian chants. Christian hope is not, as Karl Marx wrongly suggested, a fleeing from the earth and a longing beyond history. Rather, Christian hope is a way of life on earth and in history in obedience to the call to discipleship. After all, if we claim to be in relationship with the incarnate, world-affirming, history-redeeming Lord Jesus Christ, we might well expect that that relationship would lead us to participate through the Holy Spirit in his continuing redemption of the evils under which his people live and die.

The contemporary German theologian Jürgen Moltmann has argued in a number of books that all theology is by necessity political theology: theology done in the context of murder, torture, starvation, and death. Similarly, all Christian life is inherently political. To hope in Christ means we will no longer put up with reality as it is. The coming reign of God is a provocation that criticizes every unfulfilled present. Hope that is in Christ draws the mind into opposition to existing reality, which has no truth in it, provoking a peculiar incongruence with the status quo and setting loose powers that are critical and transformative. The person of faith suffers under the difference between hope and reality, refusing to be reconciled to evil, no longer willing to tolerate it. As people of hope, Christians cannot resign from the world. Thus Moltmann wrote that "those who hope in Christ can no longer put up with reality as it is, but begin to suffer under it, to contradict it. Peace with God means conflict with the world, for the goad of the promised future stabs inexorably into the flesh of every unfulfilled present."[3]

A feature of Calvin's thought is that the whole world belongs to the reign of Jesus Christ and has come under his redemption, and that the triumph of Christ will be manifest among all nations. The missionary impulse of the gospel is compelled by an inner necessity to reach forth into the present condition of humankind and cannot be limited to the reconciliation of souls to God, for God's grace in and through Jesus Christ extends over the whole world. All creation, spiritual and material, is the arena of the reign of Christ, which means that Christian hope has to be thought through in terms that include political and economic hope in the light of the reign of Christ.

Christian hope does not dissolve hope into politics. But in obedience to Christ, Christians place themselves into situations that call out for transformation. The hope of the gospel must be seen as hope for the poor and the exploited, wherever they are to be found, as well as hope for the sick and dying. Without a doubt, the people of Calle Real are deeply politicized in the strength of the gospel of Jesus Christ. They take sides in the great debates of their society. Expressions of hope by necessity are bound up with contingent process, party political issues, economic analyses, and contemporary political debates, for real life demands such engagement. A ministry of hope that does not risk concrete engagement ultimately fails to be a ministry of hope, instead becoming a faithless sitting on the sideline for fear of contamination.

Christians, acting in hope, will seek rather to anticipate the future of Christ according to the measure of the possibilities available to them. Faithfulness always means the risk of involvement. Even so, we suggest a caveat, for a politics of Christian hope will also be a theology of hope that refuses to ratify any political and economic program or process as in itself the complete will of God. The reign of God involves liberation for the poor, but liberation for the poor is not yet the reign of God. To say otherwise is idolatry, calling into question the singular Lordship of Jesus Christ over all political systems and ideologies. Even while working within the possibilities of politics, Christians inspired by the hope of the gospel will not grant supreme obedience to any nation, culture, or political philosophy. A gospel proviso does not allow us too close a connection between the gospel and any country or nationality, or any political or economic philosophy. While the politics of freedom and democracy have a moral force unequalled in human experience, the reign of God is never to be collapsed into these political ideas and expressions.

In conclusion, consider God's name, which God gave to Moses: "I AM WHO I AM." (Exodus 3:14) Moses' question concerning the meaning of the name of God is really an inquiry into the relationship between God and God's people. The profoundly practical question that Moses puts to God does not so much concern God's transcendent 'I-ness' as such, but God's faithfulness. The divine name is not a mere repetition. Rather, the answer tells Moses that God is a God of the future, and not only of the past (of Abraham, Isaac, and Jacob, Ex. 3:6). The revelation of the name is the giving of a promise, the fulfillment of which is God's surety for the future. Israel learned who God will be. Whatever else the name means, it also refers to the promise of the ineffable presence of God with the people as God journeys ahead of them, leading and preparing the way into their coming future with God. On the basis of this God we have hope for a coming future that is God's making, which is no less than a new heaven and a new earth.

17

The Joy of Faith

What do we mean when as Christians we speak about joy? In what way is it more than a good feeling and an upbeat mood? Something of the depth of joy is seen in a story from my own family. My dear mother loved to tell this story about perhaps the single happiest moment of her life. She had not been long married when my father was called to fight in Burma under Lord Mountbatten in the Second World War. My father rarely spoke later of his four years in the jungle. Living with the reality and fear of quick and violent death was too terrible a memory to discuss. He knew of my mother's loneliness and anxiety as she waited at home, praying for his safe return. Communication was rare; my mother would go for long periods with no word from my father. After the defeat of Japan, my father was shipped home in the early winter of 1945, though my mother had no certain knowledge of his situation or condition.

One morning she was in the neighborhood butcher shop in Edinburgh when she heard shouting in the street. She went to the door and saw people leaning out of the open tenement windows applauding. Turning her head up the street, she beheld her husband, home from the war, striding proudly down the middle of the road on his way to find her.

My mother dropped her shopping where she stood, screamed out my father's name, and ran wildly to embrace him. By now the whole street was cheering the joyous homecoming. For my mother on that glorious day, joy had a name. It was "Jimmy"—her husband, my father. Joy can be such an explosion of glorious human emotion. But even a wonderful story does not say the last word about joy.

At John 15:11, Jesus says to his hearers, "I have said these things to you so that my joy may be in you, and that your joy may be complete." The joy of faith completes our human joys, adding something beyond what even the most blessed joys of human love can give. The joy of faith does not mean that our human joys do not really matter to God; rather, the joy of faith adds a dimension to joy hitherto both unknown and unavailable outside of relationship with God.

Joy, a little one-syllable word, hardly seems sturdy enough to carry the full weight of Christian fulfillment. How easily the word just slips by, apparently adding little to the full understanding and experience of faith. We then must lay out a theological case for faith's experience of a joy that is more than the world's pleasure.

According to Psalm 30:5, "Weeping may linger for the night, but joy comes with the morning." In the Hebrew text, the word for joy (*rinnah*) means "loud crying out," "proclamation," or "singing." The best way to render the text is indeed: "Weeping may linger for the night, but **JOY** comes with the morning." Joy: loud, assertive, as powerful as the transition from darkness to daybreak, from death to life.

Psalm 30 is a thanksgiving psalm that tells the story of going into trouble and coming out of trouble.[1] We do not know the physical problem faced by the psalmist, but it is described in imagery of death and survival—serious stuff indeed. In the face of death, the psalmist praises God for what amounts to a resurrection experience: You, God, have drawn me up, healed me, lifted me up from death, restored me to life. At verse 4 the psalmist invites everyone else now to praise God, for such praise cannot be contained within one individual. Sing praises, give thanks to God for God has overcome whatever trouble was visited upon the psalmist. What previously felt like the dead of night now feels like the joy of sunrise. The transition from death to life is as the move from night to morning. The spiritual autobiography of the psalmist progresses from feeling good to the pit of death to new life. New life calls for praise; silence is impossible. The psalmist ends with thanksgiving: O Lord my God, I will give thanks to you forever.

This word for joy at Psalm 30:5 is used rarely in the Old Testament. We find it also at Psalm 126:6: those who go out weeping, bearing the seeds for sowing, shall come home with shouts of joy, carrying their sheaves. Or as the Christian song puts it: "Going forth with weeping, sowing for the Master, Tho' the loss sustained our spirit often grieves; when our weeping's over, He will bid us welcome, we shall come rejoicing, bringing in the sheaves."[2]

Jesus has his own version of these psalm themes: "Very truly, I tell you, you will weep and mourn, but the world will rejoice; you will have pain, but your pain will turn into joy. . . . no one will take your joy from you." (John 16:20, 22) Joy is the expression of a profound inner disposition of gratitude to God that may be expressed in shouts of joy, crashing cymbals, loud singing of "hallelujah." However expressed, this joy is given from beyond the finite limits of earthly possibility. Christian joy is a joy that has a sole basis in what God has done to redeem the human situation. People who sow in tears shall reap with songs of joy because God brings life out of death.

Obstacles to Joy

Joy—how unusual that word sounds to Protestant ears! African American and charismatic Christians aside, adherents to Reformed faith especially are not usually noted for their particularly joyful expression of Christian faith. To take the example of Presbyterians, the term "dour" never seems to modify anyone but the Scots, and by implication, Presbyterianism. True to form, the *Encyclopedia of the Reformed Faith* (ed. D. M. McKim) includes no entry under joy, and only one footnote entry for joy is present in the whole of Calvin's *Institutes*. A good reason for our reputation apparently exists. Is a joyful Protestant a contradiction? Perhaps we are rightfully fearful of turning Christian joy into a superficial kind of cheeriness, into a good mood. After all, the experience of God's redemption is more than the feeling of having a good day. Nevertheless, if we are not joyful, how can we speak of ourselves as the people of God, as the people whom God has turned from death to life, from night to the morning of the new day?

The question might also be posed: How can we properly feel joy in a world with so much terrible suffering? The newspaper headlines with their dire reports frequently disturb any sense of well being we may have in the morning. What right does one have to reflect upon joy amid terrifying earthquakes and the continuing ravages of war, the death of children from random acts of violence, and the blight of untreatable diseases? What place can be found for joy for those with Alzheimer's disease, when the mind has almost completely failed and dearly loved ones go unrecognized? What case can be made for joy in the cancer wards of children's hospitals? Feeling joy has both theological and emotional dimensions. Given the litany of pain and evil at every turn, should not our lives be lived in moral outrage against a God who would create and allow such sorrow rather than living in the joy of faith?

These two questions also have raw emotional power. We are very much aware obviously that we feel our own pain and the assault of evil upon us. Fear lurks ready to pounce at every twinge in our bodies, and at the threat of attack and criticism. An awareness of our own capacity for sin seems also to increase as we grow older. Maturity in grace increases our personal sense of sinfulness. The suffering of those whom we love is likewise a huge emotional burden. But also we feel—or at least we have some sensitivity towards—the tragedies and disasters that befall others, indeed millions of people quite unknown to us. In the face of such overwhelming suffering, shutting down the capacity to feel pain is perhaps easier than living in heightened awareness.

Clearly, the case that must be made for the joy of faith has very real obstacles to overcome. Honesty teaches us that we and those we love will suffer. A faith and a spirituality that does not allow us to enter into the terrible mystery of the death of our children and the murder of our loved ones; that does not help us embrace the moral failure of the genocides and abandonings that scar the face of history; that does not enable us to face the profound loneliness and fear of our darkest experience, at least on occasion, would be a false faith and a worthless spirituality. Any joy of faith worth having must face up to and deal with the horror that presses upon us. If joy is to be more than whistling in the dark whenever we feel alone and afraid—a phony cheeriness to keep our spirits up—then it must face these forces that seek to destroy us. The faith that leads to joy must enable us to confront the darkness unto death as not having the last word.

Sharing in the Joy of Jesus Christ

Following the biblical pattern, a specifically Christian account of joy grounds our joy in Jesus Christ. In Luke, for example, the

Christian gospel of God's redemption in Jesus Christ is cradled, beginning to end, by joy. The message of salvation is announced to the shepherds by the angel of the Lord: "Do not be afraid; for see—I am bringing you good news of great joy for all the people." (Luke 2:10) In the beginning there is joy—indeed, great joy—because Jesus' birth is good news. Joy is the key signature of the gospel, the consequence of its reality, the characteristic of gospel faith. After the ascension, now at the end of the story, Luke tells us that the disciples worshiped Jesus and went on their way back to Jerusalem, again with great joy (Luke 24:52), because the Lord Jesus reigns and rules. In Matthew, joy is associated with the women's experience at the empty tomb when the angel announced the message of the risen Lord (28:8), because Jesus overcomes evil and death and is now alive for evermore. Joy has its source in Jesus. He is our joy: who he is and what he has done for us. The birth, death, resurrection, and ascension of our Lord are the grounds and the occasion for the Christian's joy. Joy is the consequence of knowing Jesus and living our lives in him.

What is this Christian joy? We turn to John 15:11 for a closer analysis in order to deepen our understanding. "I have said these things to you," says Jesus, of the teaching on abiding in him and of being attached to the true vine, "so that my joy may be in you, and that your joy may be complete." This verse has extraordinary theological implications for a proper understanding of the joy of faith. Through this verse, we can explore the meaning of Jesus' joy in his own relationship with the Father, return to the doctrine of our union with Christ as the way by which we share in his joy and show how this sharing in our Lord's joy completes our joy.

First of all, the verse refers to Jesus' joy. The text states that Jesus spoke of "my joy." For Jesus, joy was undoubtedly a profoundly personal and intimate experience, and it was more than happiness. Because of who he was, Jesus' joy was more profoundly the expression of his intrinsic interior reality, of his unique being as the Son of God. His joy was the consequence of his unbroken communion with the Father, a communion that constituted his being as Emmanuel. Jesus' joy was the result of the internal relation of his own being as the incarnate Son to the one being of the living God. Because in his innermost being he was the Son of God, God of God and Light of Light, as the Creed puts it, his life was lived out in the joy of communion with God. Even on the cross, when he struggled mightily with his sense of abandonment and dereliction, he could still end with an affirmation of trust in who he was and what he was about: "Father, into your hands I commend my spirit." (Luke 23:46) His joy points us profoundly and unmistakably into the deepest life of and relationships within the Holy Trinity. In practical terms, Jesus' joy was expressed in his keeping of his Father's commandments and his abiding in his Father's love.

Second, this intimate union with the Father that is the source of Jesus' joy is the gift that he now shares with those who love him: no less than salvation. Jesus' gift is to let us into his own relationship with his Father through our union with him. His will is that he shares this relationship, that he gives it away to his disciples. And for what reason does he do this? The answer is found at John 15:11, "that my joy may be in you," and as he prays at John 17:13, "that they"—the disciples, and you and me—"may have my joy made complete in themselves." How wonderful that Jesus' will is for us to be joyful by being filled with the joy that is his. Our joy lies in the gift he gives us of his own deepest intimacy with God through our union with him. The joy that is his by nature becomes ours by grace.

Third, John 15:11 tells us also that this gift completes our joy. Christian joy does not obliterate our humanity, with its many little but important joys. Our joy with family, in sport played and watched, in the mystery of a good meal with dear friends, in satisfying work done well (fill in your own joys as you wish) . . . these moments are not of little value. Who we are and what we are about matter eternally to God. Christian joy means the discovery of our humanity in its fullest, not the loss of self but the coming home to ourselves in a quite remarkable way, to discover our true selves as we are in Christ. As our Lord's joy expressed itself in obedience and love, so too our union with him will express itself with joy in acts of obedience and love. Note again the critical point: our joy flows from our union with Jesus Christ, from our being ultimately and intimately grounded in a personal relationship with him, just as his joy flows from his union with the Father.

These three points may be summarized as follows: The joy of the Christian is not a mere feeling of happiness, nor does Christian joy have much to do with cheeriness. Christian joy is the result of our union with Christ. As Christians we are so bonded into Jesus through the work of the Holy Spirit that we share in the Lord's inner communion with the Father. Our joy is experientially, as the hymn puts it, "a foretaste of glory divine," or as the great Eastern Orthodox tradition puts it, no less than of union with God.

Joy and the Cross

We turn now finally to consider a deep mystery at the heart of Christian joy, namely, the relationship between the cross and joy. Christian joy does not mean happiness because we have avoided or survived suffering and sorrow. Joy is a deeper and more subtle thing, more than an emotion. Joy is a state of faith in which fullness and peace and confidence in God in and through suffering and sorrow are present. We find a clue about this joy at Hebrews 12:2, where the writer tells us that Jesus "who for the sake of the joy that was set before him endured the cross." The journey to the cross was not a course he took for himself alone, but a course he took for us and for our salvation. His joy was that he took on the sins of the whole world as the means of redemption. This act was the fulfillment of his innermost being as the Son of the Father, as Emmanuel, as God with us and God for us.

Jesus did not take a masochistic delight in suffering—such a view would be both ridiculous and blasphemous, as is the view that the Father required an equivalent suffering to atone for human sin. Rather, in the deepest sense imaginable, Christ's joy, the fullest expression of his profound union with the Father, and of the Father's love for us (see John 3:16), was his atonement, his at-one-ment with our plight and his bearing of its consequence on the cross of Calvary. Jesus' deepest joy was not found in the avoidance of his cross, as much as that was humanly desirable (Luke 22:42). In a manner that utterly transcends our sense of joy as a mere emotion or cheerfulness, Jesus found his deepest joy in enduring the cross for what that suffering meant in his service of God and of you and me, his brothers and sisters. His joy at the end on the cross surely had to do with his completion of his life on earth as the one who in his death gave life to the whole world. The cross is not the failure and the resurrection the victory. The cross is itself the victory, and the resurrection—that is, life—is its consequence.

Christian joy is not to be found in the absence of suffering, but in the light that shines forever out of the deepest and darkest pit of gloom. Reflecting on John 16:20, and in words that are fraught with mystery, William Temple, the late Archbishop of Canterbury, suggests not only that joy will take the place of sorrow, but also that sorrow itself becomes the joy, because the Cross of Christ is the triumph. In that event sorrow becomes joy through the mystery of the Lord's defeat of evil at its worst.[3]

One way to speak of this transformation is to say that the joy of faith involves living in the light of an alternative understanding of reality, an understanding built entirely on the victory of Jesus Christ rather than on the 'realism' of the tragedies of history. The hope of the gospel, and the only real basis for joy, is that God in and through Jesus Christ has entered into the darkness of our plight unto death and brought light and life to bear for us, a light and a life that the darkness of evil and death cannot overcome, and that we share through the grace of the Holy Spirit. The basis of Christian joy lies in the fact that through the Holy Spirit the incarnate Savior has given us his victory and therefore his joy. He has poured himself into us. Says Paul, "it is no longer I who live, but it is Christ who lives in me." (Gal. 2:20) The search for Christian joy does not in the end cast us back upon our selves in the hope of finding a full reservoir of upbeat emotional energy. Rather the quest directs us to Jesus and the life he now lives in us in the power of the Holy Spirit, a life by which we in him share with joy in his intimate union with the Father. Christian joy has a name: Jesus Christ our Lord.

Acknowledgments

The incentive to complete this book was provided by a gift from Signal Mountain Presbyterian Church, Signal Mountain, Tennessee. We express our gratitude to that congregation, and especially to the senior pastor, Dr. William Dudley, and the mission chairman, Don Hofmann. We also acknowledge with appreciation the encouragement of our friend Betty Moore of Florence, South Carolina.

Charles Partee would like to express his gratitude to God for the communities of faith in which he has lived and learned: The Presbyterian churches of Brinkley, Arkansas; Marvell, Arkansas; Frenchtown, New Jersey; and Shadyside of Pittsburgh. And for three special friends: Donald Gene McGarity, Douglas S. Pride, and Calvin C. Wilson. We are surrounded by a great cloud of witnesses.

Andrew Purves would like to express his gratitude to and affection for the annual Christian Life Conference and the annual Wee Kirk Conference, both held at the Montreat Conference Center, Montreat, North Carolina. The invitations through the years to speak at these conferences have been an enormous encouragement. And to the members of the Order of St. Peter, past and present, for their prayers, their love for a brother in Christ, and their affirmation of his ministry as a teacher of the Christian faith.

Notes

Calvin's *Institutes*, cited in the Library of Christian Classics edition, is referenced by book, chapter, and paragraph. John Calvin, *Institutes of the Christian Religion*, ed. John T. McNeill, trans. Ford Lewis Battles, 2 vols. (Philadelphia: The Westminster Press, 1960).

The most recent available English translations of Calvin's biblical commentaries are cited by book, chapter, and verse. *Commentaries of John Calvin*, various translators, 46 vols. (Edinburgh: The Calvin Translation Society, 1843–1855). *Calvin's New Testament Commentaries*, ed. David W. Torrance and Thomas F. Torrance, various translators, 12 vols. (Grand Rapids: William B. Eerdmans, 1959–1972).

Chapter 1

1. *The Confessions of St. Augustine*, VIII.12.29, various translations.
2. For a careful and important exposition of convictional knowing see James E. Loder, *The Transforming Moment*, 2nd ed. (Colorado Springs: Helmers & Howard, 1989).
3. Kant based his ethics on the mystery of the transcendental 'ought.'
4. Karl Jaspers, *Kerygma & Myth: A Theological Debate*, ed. Hans-Werner Bartsch, trans. Reginald H. Fuller (London: SPCK, 1972), 133.

Chapter 2

1. This formulation is found in James B. Torrance, *Worship, Community and the Triune God of Grace* (Carlisle, U.K.: Paternoster Press, 1996).
2. Commentary on 1 Corinthians 11:24.
3. Karl Barth, *Church Dogmatics*, ed. G. W. Bromiley and T. F. Torrance (Edinburgh: T. & T. Clark, 1957), II.1, 149.

Chapter 3

1. Thomas F. Torrance, *The Christian Doctrine of God: One Being, Three Persons* (Edinburgh: T. & T. Clark, 1996), 56.

173

2. Thus, Friederich Schleiermacher in *The Christian Faith* 2 vols. (New York: Harper & Row Torchbooks, 1963), where the doctrine of the Trinity is treated at the very end of his systematic theology.

3. See Karl Barth, *Church Dogmatics*, ed. G. W. Bromiley and T. F. Torrance (Edinburgh: T. & T. Clark, 1957), II.1, 229f.

Chapter 4

1. The recent linguistic conviction that the word "man" excludes women distorts the traditional and orthodox Christological claim. That is, when Jesus was called "God," the term was not being used as an abstract noun (deity) but as a personal name. Jesus was being given the name of God with us (Emmanuel). The term "man" was formerly understood to refer to both a man and all humankind. In the doctrine of the hypostatic union Jesus was understood to be fully God and fully an individual man and also to represent all people before God. With the terms Deity and Humanity, Divine and Human, God and Human, etc., a serious effort must be made to understand the meaning of the church's original confession. The present linguistic preferences actually seem to disguise the theological issue of particularity and universality in the humanity of Christ. Being named God and being called divine are not obviously equivalent. Certainly being human and symbolizing humanity before God is not the same as really being a man, who is also really God, and therefore is able to unite us to himself and to God at the same time.

2. Thomas F. Torrance, *The Christian Doctrine of God: One Being, Three Persons* (Edinburgh: T. & T. Clark, 1996), 51.

3. Helmut Thielicke, *The Evangelical Faith, Vol. 2: The Doctrine of God and of Christ*, ed. and trans. G. W. Bromiley (Grand Rapids: William B. Eerdmans, 1977), 358.

4. "Christ takes up what has been prophesied in the offices and also breaks it. He both fulfils and transcends it." *Ibid.*, 360.

5. T. W. Manson, *Ministry and Priesthood: Christ's and Ours* (Richmond: John Knox Press, 1958), 31. John Calvin, in his *Institutes*, held together the person and work of Christ, and developed the threefold office of prophet, priest, and king, in that order, although the priestly office was usually given priority in the way the offices were developed. The emphasis was on his offices "for us." This Reformed use of the threefold offices of Christ, and especially of his priestly office, has a biblical basis, though best understood not as a pure biblical theology as such, but as a Church theology that enables us to grasp the person and work of Jesus in a helpful way.

Chapter 5

1. One of the most important early texts on the Holy Spirit makes the point quite simply: "His first and most proper title is Holy Spirit," St. Basil the Great, *On the Holy Spirit*, trans. D. Anderson, (Crestwood, N.Y.: St. Vladimir's Seminary Press, 1980), 9.22, 42.

2. Karl Barth, *Church Dogmatics* IV.2, ed. G. W. Bromiley and T. F. Torrance (Edinburgh: T. & T. Clark, 1958), 323.

3. This language is taken from James B. Torrance, *Worship, Community and the Triune God of Grace*.

4. Barth, *Church Dogmatics* IV.2 *op. cit.*, 324.

5. George S. Hendry, *The Holy Spirit in Christian Theology* (Philadelphia: The Westminster Press, 1956), 22.

6. Ray S. Anderson, *Ministry on the Fireline: A Practical Theology for an Empowered Church* (Downers Grove, Ill: Inter-Varsity Press, 1993), 40.

7. Ibid., 30–31.

8. Ibid., 33.

9. Hendry, *op. cit.*, 23.

10. Ibid., 27.

11. Anderson, *op. cit.*, 22.

12. Karl Barth, *Church Dogmatics* IV.2, *op. cit.*, 322.

13. For a discussion, see Charles Partee, "Calvin's Central Dogma Again," *The Sixteenth-Century Journal* 18, no. 2 (Summer 1987): 191f.

14. For a discussion, see T. F. Torrance, *The Christian Doctrine of God: One Being, Three Persons* (Edinburgh: T. & T. Clark, 1996), 102.

15. See Andrew Purves and Mark Achtemeier, *Union in Christ* (Louisville, Ky.: Witherspoon Press, 1999), 43.

16. *The Scots Confession of 1560: A Modern Translation by James Bulloch* (Edinburgh: The Saint Andrew Press, 1960), 1.

Chapter 6

1. *The Presbyterian Enterprise: Sources of American Presbyterian History*, ed. Maurice W. Armstrong, Lefferts A. Loetscher, and Charles A. Anderson (Philadelphia: The Westminster Press, 1956), 286.

Chapter 7

1. John McLeod Campbell, *The Nature of the Atonement* (Edinburgh & Grand Rapids: Wm. B. Eerdmans, 1996), 45. For a discussion see Thomas F. Torrance, *Scottish Theology: From John Knox to John McLeod Campbell* (Edinburgh: T. & T. Clark, 1996), 287f.

2. The interchange of 'many' and 'all' in these verses is a matter of enduring debate. Arguably, 'many' means 'all', in which case, Paul is cast into the universalist camp; but that does not fit tidily with the judgment themes found, for example, at Romans 1. There remains the irresolvable tension between verse 15 ('many') and verse 18 ('all'), suggesting perhaps a real tension in Paul himself on this point, a tension that he did not care to resolve one way or the other. The same tension is found also at 1 Corinthians 15:22–23, where Paul again used the Adam-Christ typology.

3. Eugene H. Peterson, *The Message: The New Testament in Contemporary English* (Colorado Springs, Colorado: NavPress, 1993), 314.

4. Karl Barth, *Church Dogmatics* IV.2, ed. G. W. Bromiley and T. F. Torrance (Edinburgh: T. & T. Clark, 1958), 516.

Chapter 8

1. Karl Barth, *Church Dogmatics I.1: The Doctrine of the Word of God*, ed. G. W. Bromiley and T. F. Torrance (Edinburgh: T. & T. Clark, 1975), 55.

Chapter 9

1. Karl Barth, *Church Dogmatics* IV.2, ed. G. W. Bromiley and T. F. Torrance (Edinburgh: T. & T. Clark, 1958), 518.
2. James S. Stewart, *A Man in Christ: the Vital Elements of St. Paul's Religion* (New York: Harpers, n.d.), 147.

Chapter 11

1. W. Somerset Maugham, "Sheppey," *The Collected Plays* III (London: William Heinemann, Ltd., 1961 [1931]), 298.

Chapter 12

1. Commentary on Ephesians 6:8.
2. John A. T. Robinson, *Honest to God* (Philadelphia: Westminster Press, 1963), 19–20.
3. Commentary on Matthew 21:21.
4. Friedrich Heiler, *Prayer, A Study in the History and Psychology of Religion*, trans. Samuel McComb (London: Oxford University, 1932), 92.
5. Mark Twain, *The Adventures of Huckleberry Finn* (New York: Rinehart, 1948), chap. 3.
6. Louis Bouyer, *Introduction to Spirituality*, trans. Mary Perkins Ryan (New York: Desclee, 1961), 59.
7. John Calvin, *Institution of the Christian Religion* (1536). (Atlanta: John Knox Press, 1975), 108.
8. Commentary on Matthew 6:8.
9. Commentary on Philippians 2:13.
10. Ibid.
11. Commentary on Psalm 10:13.
12. Commentary on 2 Corinthians 12:8.
13. Commentary on Jeremiah 29:12.
14. Commentary on John 16:26.

Chapter 13

1. See James Smart, *The Strange Silence of the Bible in the Church* (Philadelphia: Westminster Press, 1970).
2. The Presbyterian Church (U.S.A.), *The Book of Confessions*, "The Confession of 1967," 9:29–30.

Chapter 14

1. Cited by Lyall Watson in *Dark Nature: A Natural History of Evil* (New York: Harper Collins, 1995), 5–6.

2. John Calvin, *Letters 1528–1545*, part 1, ed. Jules Bonnet, trans. David Constable (Grand Rapids: Baker Book House, 1983 [1858]), 344.

3. John Bright, *A History of Israel* (London: SCM Press, 1970), 331.

4. Walter Brueggemann, *The Message of the Psalms: A Theological Commentary* (Minneapolis: Augsburg Publishing House, 1984), 75.

5. Ibid., 77.

6. Henri Nouwen, *The Wounded Healer* (Garden City, N.Y.: Doubleday & Co., 1972), 73.

Chapter 15

1. See Richard H. Popkin's *The History of Skepticism from Erasmus to Spinoza* (Berkeley: Univ. of California, 1979).

2. Commentary on Ephesians 8:33–34. Emphases added.

3. ST I.II. quest. 112, art. 5; but see II.II quest. 18. art. 4.

4. Council of Trent, Chapter XI.

5. Martin Luther, *On the Bondage of the Will*, trans. J. I. Packer and O. R. Johnston. (Westwood, N.J.: Fleming H. Revell, 1957), 124.

6. *Documents of the Christian Church*, ed. Henry Bettenson (New York: Oxford University Press, 1943), 285.

7. Council of Trent, Chapter IX.

8. Allan Bloom, *The Closing of the American Mind* (New York: Simon and Schuster, 1987), 25–26.

9. Luther, op. cit., 314. Emphasis added.

10. Commentary on Mark 9:24.

11. Commentary on Psalm 22:2.

12. Ibid., 3:19.

13. Emil Brunner, *Truth as Encounter* (Philadelphia: The Westminster Press, 1964), 66.

Chapter 16

1. *Book of Common Worship* (Louisville, Ky.: Westminster/John Knox Press, 1993), 925.

2. Elie Wiesel, *Night* (Harmondsworth, England: Penguin Books, 1960), 76–77.

3. Jürgen Moltmann, *Theology of Hope* (London: SCM Press, 1967), 21.

Chapter 17

1. For a discussion see Walter Brueggemann, *The Message of the Psalms* (Minneapolis: Augsburg Publishing House, 1984), 126.

2. Words written by Knowles Shaw in 1874 and music written by George A. Minor in 1880.

3. See William Temple, *Readings in St. John's Gospel* (Wilton, CT: Morehouse Barlow Co., 1985), 282.